||| || ||||||| ||| || |||||||||||| |||| |||
⬦ **W9-BNT-398**

LIFE IS A GAME

. . . and you can play it!

LIFE IS A GAME
...and you can play it.

23 Essential lessons
for living your best life.

What If. . ?
...a challenge, a possible future

BY "NANCY B" BERGGREN

Literary Press

Newport Beach, CA

www.literarypress.com

*Reprinted by permission of Atria Books, an imprint of Simon & Schuster Adult Publishing
Group from TOMORROW'S GOD by Neale Donald Walsch.*

Library of Congress control number: 2005924454
ISBN 0-9764765-1-7

FIRST EDITION
Printed in the United States of America

www.LifeisaGame-whatif.com

This book is dedicated to
Mother and Dad,
who taught me to love;
to Dick,
whose wisdom, strength, and faith
gave me wings to fly;
and to Steve, Lisa, Linda, and Scott,
who fill my life with joy.

CONTENTS

PREFACE

Mother said I popped out with a Southern drawl, so when her sister (who basically raised her) said she needed to take me to her son's acting teacher to get rid of it, she did as she was told. Thus, at two-and-a-half, I was introduced to a world of magic, where I could do anything, be anything far grander, bigger, and greater than my small self ever could be.

Drama, comedy, music, dance, it all came so naturally to me—it was what I was born to do. The joy of performing and the freedom I felt onstage poured out through me like a river overflowing with so much love, I sometimes felt like I would burst. Why I never became the next Shirley Temple, I never quite figured out—*and it really ticks me off*—but I'm working on it!

But here's the real kicker. While I was given carte blanche to laugh, cry, scream, argue, hit, strut, manipulate, whine, and beg, *onstage*, I was basically supposed to be invisible *offstage*. Be quiet, sit on the chair, keep your skirt down, and for heaven sake, don't call any attention to yourself, or think you are anything special! Express only love, and when you can't do that, stay in your room until you can!

I can understand the motives behind it. At that time, my mother had an almost paralyzing inferiority complex, and she loathed Hollywood brats and their pushy mothers and was determined that we would be neither. But as an impressionable child actress who desperately needed her mother's approval, I felt loved only when I got the part, emoted fully for the director, and then managed to stay invisible the rest of the time.

This dichotomy became so deeply entrenched in me that when I went to the Lee Strasberg Institute in Hollywood for acting classes as an adult, I couldn't identify my own emotions. I didn't know whether I was depressed, frustrated, angry, jealous, confused, conflicted, or whatever. It was impossible for me to ask for what I wanted, or to stand up for myself in any way. By this time, not only did I not think I was anything *special*, I guess I really thought I was nothing at all. As a result of feeling so deeply unworthy, I often sabotaged my greatest opportunities, the fruits of a lifetime of intense and dedicated study in the craft that I loved.

The final blow came when I managed to sabotage a recurring role on *Dynasty*—my greatest theatrical coup to date. It is still painful to recall, and I feel deeply ashamed of my behavior at that time, which is so diametrically opposed to who I am today. I chose to share it here because it so clearly illustrates the power of our childhood experiences and how they can affect us subconsciously throughout our lives. It also points out the gifts hidden within our most painful and challenging trials.

The first day on the set was heaven! Everything went smoothly. Everyone, including the stars, were friendly and helpful, and I went home walking on air! I had finally arrived!

If the first day was heaven, the second day was hell! They had allowed half as much time for hair and makeup, but I felt uncomfortable with it, so I came earlier—so early that I sat in my car to read and meditate. When I walked in, still earlier than my call time, they jumped all over me, saying that I was late, and that they were waiting for me on the set! I was appalled and terrified, and assured them that I had arrived at the call time I'd been given.

That put the young man who signed us out the night before in trouble, and while I felt sorry for him, I put it behind me and rushed to get to the set as quickly as possible.

Hours later, when I had time to rest in my dressing room, I casually reached into my bag for the timesheet to reassure myself that I had been right. However, to my *horror* I discovered that *I was wrong*! The young man in question had given me a time change, and I *was* to have been there an hour earlier, just as he kept stating so vehemently all day long.

Not so bad, you say? Not the end of the world—*unless* you already felt unworthy and this just confirmed it! Unless you were terrified to admit you'd *made a mistake*—since you had to be *perfect* to deserve love. Unless you feared the loss of approval (Mother again). Instead of going straight to the director with the timesheet in hand and apologizing to the young man, thus feeling forgiven and FREE to complete my scenes for the day, I tried to "stuff it" (*but it would not stuff*)! Everyplace I looked the victim of my lie by omission fell within my gaze. Suddenly I felt ugly, exposed, and a liar (he knew my guilty secret), and I found myself in a living hell—*of my own making*!

If it hadn't mattered to me that someone was being punished unfairly because of me, it would not have affected me. The truth was that I cared deeply, but the fear in me was almost paralyzing (Mom again?) and I could not overcome it. I could not make myself speak up.

When I got home, I called the assistant director and told her I had found the timesheet and apologized, but it was too late. The damage had been done. My guilt and fear had so consumed me that it had affected my performance (how could it not?), and they never used me again.

That's when I quit the business. I had sabotaged myself before, but never so shamefully, and I determined that I had done it for the very last time. I reasoned that if this was what I'd been working toward my whole life, and I had allowed this uncontrollable fear to rob me of my dream, it must not have been what I really wanted. Today, I can say that I am grateful for the lessons this experience taught me, but at the time, all I felt was shame, guilt, and devastating loss.

I turned away from the industry I loved and threw myself into my spiritual studies. I had to know why such unrealistic fears kept me prisoner, and how to release them. Thus began my quest for the Rules of the Game of Life, although I did not know it at the time. Now, years later, I can honestly say *I am free* and feel the truth of it resonate in my heart, having experienced great success in many areas of my life and career. Among the most joyful has been the privilege of sharing these simple truths with others and watching them transform their lives, reach their goals, live their dreams, and learn to forgive and love themselves...just the way they are. The big surprise is that I find myself being drawn back to my first love, the theatre; letting the love in my heart that is so much bigger than I, coupled with my God-given talents and abilities, pour out to touch, inspire, and lift up others.

So, what's the gift? If you haven't figured it out by now, it's this: love, kindness, compassion, generosity, and honesty are the ground of our being, the very fabric of our souls, and *nothing* can long succeed without it—not health, not wealth, not relationships, not happiness. When we operate against our basic values, against who and what we really are at our core, sooner or later we will destroy ourselves. It's taken years of counseling, study, and self-forgiveness to stand in my truth today, to tell it like it is, and to hold myself accountable when I mess up.

I am writing this book for two reasons: first, to share some of my own life's lessons—some difficult, some miraculous, and some downright sidesplitting hilarious; and, second, to tell you that when you mess up (and you will, because it's only human and everybody does it), it's OK, because it teaches us humility and some of the most important truths life has to offer.

In hindsight, we can all usually find some good, some deeper understanding gained from our challenges. I am suggesting that instead of waiting ten or twenty years to find the good that we begin to claim it while we are in the middle of the muddle! If there is good in it ten years from now, there is good in it now! It takes training ourselves to think in an entirely new way, but the effort is well worth the peace of mind we gain, and the greater ease with which we move through life's inevitable ups and downs.

Finally, you deserve love just because of who you are, a unique and irreplaceable creation of the one Creator, and not because of what you do. *LIFE is a GAME*, full of mystery, gifts, and surprises. Not all of them will look like what we would choose, but if we can trust our instincts, our "still small voice" that always knows what is right, and let love lead the way, we will come out winners in the end. I know it, because I can honestly say today that I'm a winner—and so are you!

ACKNOWLEDGMENTS

"In the beginning" was the Presence, the Infinite Creator in me, without whom not a single word would have been written. Each day I continue to receive guidance regarding my next steps, and I am humbled and grateful to be used by the Divine in this way.

To my current prayer partners—Esther Jones and Karen Wiley—whose constant reminders of who and what I am keep me grounded and connected to the Source of all wisdom, and creativity. They listen with their hearts, never judge, and always believe.

To my Master Mind Group, Esther, Bill Hansen, and John Prieskorn—who walked with me and supported my vision for the future through the most challenging years of my life.

To all my dear Fallbrook friends, too many to mention—but especially Nikki Hale, Ruthann and Joel Banner, Rev. Michael Summers, Shade Law, Lorea Herald, and Elizabeth Roberts—who gave me the opportunity to discover how to be a place through which the Spirit pours its great Love and Joy without end.

Very special thanks to Elizabeth Roberts, whose editing expertise helped to make sense of the beginnings of this book, and whose friendship I cherish.

To all of my colleagues and friends whose comments helped to shape the final edit.

To the authors whose insights grace the quotes included in these pages.

To Neale Donald Walsch and *Tomorrow's God* for inspiring the Prologue, *What if?* I would not change a single word, for it was indeed a message straight from the Divine. The words are not mine. They came *through* me but not *from* me; therefore, they do not belong to me—rather they belong to the world.

To all of you who have walked this spiritual path with me: Your presence, inspiration, and unfailing support are woven into the warp and woof of every page. Some word, thought, or prayer time together has helped to mold my life and contribute to who I am today.

To Robert Woodcox, who guided me to the right people at the right time to bring this book into form.

To Sharon Young, whose clarity and professional eye for detail put the polish on these pages in the final edit.

And, finally, my deepest gratitude to Richard Cheverton for creating something truly unique in both the book cover and design.

Each one of you has contributed your energy and your love to the messages contained within this book. Know that who you are and how you choose to live your life in the world makes a difference.

INTRODUCTION

This book is a walk in faith. As my friend Bill Hansen said, "It is a book to be lived." It asks you to trust in a Power greater than you are, that resides within you, that will lead you to your own answers to the questions or problems that may have plagued you for years, and prepare you for a bountiful future filled with happiness, freedom and the opportunity to fulfill your life-long dreams.

We cannot begin to heal ourselves until we are first aware that we are wounded, and then discover the root cause of that "wounded-ness." If we try to "stuff" unpleasant fears or feelings when they arise (which we have already learned doesn't work), we will never uncover their hidden cause and thus have the opportunity to heal and set ourselves free.

Through real-life examples (mine and others)—including stories of discovery, overcoming, forgiving, acceptance and release—I have offered possible solutions to some of Life's sticky problems. There are Action Steps following each Rule where you are invited to apply to your own life what has been presented on the preceding pages. You may find it helpful to read through the entire book so you can put your mind at rest about where it is leading, then go back and do the Action Steps. Take your time. Rushing through them in order to finish quickly will not afford you the time you will need to sit with the ideas presented and allow your own answers to be revealed. If one particular Rule seems to appeal the most—to jump off the page—begin there. Each Rule stands alone.

Since I believe that our Higher Power is the very Life energy within everything—the light of the stars, the warmth of the sun, our beating hearts, and our very breath—I have not chosen to limit it to only one name. Since it is limitless, infinite, and eternal, it is sometimes difficult to find a single word to describe the indescribable. Therefore, I have used several different synonyms throughout the book to attempt to capture the essence of the Divine I am feeling and writing about in any particular passage. Words such as the Divine, Higher Power, Spirit, Source, Creator, One, and others all refer to the one infinite Creator of all that is, or ever will be. If one particular synonym for the Divine is more comfortable for you, use it in place of the others.

This is your book, and it is intended to be used as a workbook. Just reading the ideas presented here, no matter how inspiring, will do nothing to change your life for the better. If you truly want to set yourself free to be all you can be, get ready to roll up your mental sleeves and get to work. No one can do this work for you. Each of us must discover our own path to healing and revealing our greatest yet-to-be for ourselves. It is available to everyone, but it is not always easy or comfortable to confront our hidden doubts or fears. However, with faith and trust in the Power greater than you are, that is right where you are, that guided your hand to this book at this time in your life, you will succeed.

The rewards will be sweet. Releasing ourselves from self-made prisons of doubt, worry, and fear frees up our Life energy to accomplish our dreams, to contribute to life that which we came here to give. Do not pressure yourself to move on to the next Rule until you are ready. If you find yourself doing deep work within one section, which is leading you to healing old wounds, stay with it until you feel complete.

Last but not least, be kind to yourself. Do not use this work to criticize, blame, or belittle yourself. Treat yourself with compassion, patience, and love. When we are learning something new, it does not always go as smoothly as we would prefer. Delving into any secret fears sometimes stirs up emotions and scenes from our past, which we have not looked at honestly or directly before. If you need to set this work aside for a time and just be with yourself until your newfound insights reveal themselves fully, please do so. The ideas presented here are meant to lift up, heal, and bless. Finally, thank yourself in advance for loving yourself enough and for having the courage and commitment to set this time aside just for you; to free yourself from any and all limitations, to be all that you came here to be.

"This is the time of Great Beginnings. It is time to die to who we used to be and to become instead who we are capable of being. This is the gift that awaits us now: the chance to become who we really are."

—Marianne Williamson, *The Gift of Change*

PROLOGUE

WHAT IF?
. . . a challenge, a possible world

"This is our aloneness
this is our time
This is the mountain we all have to climb
This is our destiny
beyond the small family
I see no boundary
between you and I."

– Miten with Deva Premal, *Into the Wind*

It was three in the morning when I was awakened with thoughts so electrifying that I hit the floor running to grab my pen and yellow pad to jot them down before they slipped away. I had been reading *Tomorrow's God* by Neale Donald Walsch, and some of the ideas were so far outside the box that they set my mind on fire. The sentence that caught me that morning and started my own creative juices flowing was...

*"Wisdom is not having all the right answers,
it is having all the right questions."*

These are, of course, God's thoughts speaking through the author of the several *Conversations with God* books.

The ideas coming through were so huge that I had to WRITE IT BIG, as our kids used to say, with sometimes only ten or twelve words on a page. As the days went by and the dialogue continued, I could not see how this information could possibly be included in *Life Is a Game*. However, when the Action Steps began to evolve, I saw how, yes, this not only could, but must be included. It is perhaps the most important part of this creative effort and the reason for writing this book in the first place.

You may have read or heard over the past few years that some kind of transformation is fast approaching that will be a quantum leap for all of humanity. Depending on what you read, or whom you listen to, it has been called many things, but in truth, no one can tell us exactly what or when it will be, because I believe we are all creating it together. It is not something being done to us, but by us. Whether we choose to go willingly and participate consciously in the coming evolutionary change, or whether we go kicking and screaming, or are even left behind, will be our ultimate individual choice.

The idea of asking the right questions seemed to open a Pandora's Box in my mind and I could hardly write fast enough to keep up with the flow. The following are, to me, some truly earth-shaking questions. I hope they will set your mind on fire with questions of your own. There are no easy answers here, no curling up with a good book comfort food. They will disturb you, anger or frighten you, and shake you up. I hope so, because we are

the ones—you and I—who are being called upon to usher in this
new millennium transformation for our children, and our children's children. I know we are up to the task, because...

now is the time,
we are here,
and there are no accidents.

What if . . . the Divine, that which we call Atman, Buddha,
Great Spirit, Allah, Yahweh, Jesus, God,
or something else, were so much greater,
so far beyond any one culture,
any one being, or group of beings'
ability to grasp and record in a Single Sacred Text,
so that none of them held the WHOLE TRUTH,
but that all of them held SOME TRUTH,
so that in order to even begin to grasp
the ALLNESS, the EVERYWHERENESS,
the within and withoutness,
of what we call the Divine, that
ALL OF THEM WERE NEEDED?

What if . . . each of them held a fragment of the whole,
like a piece of a puzzle, and
WHAT IF IT TOOK ALL OF THEM TOGETHER
to even begin to define or grasp
the scope, depth, breadth, and height of that which we call God?

What if . . . the Moslems and Bahais, Hindus and Quakers,
Mormons, Shamans, Catholics, Pagans, Jews, Spiritualists,

Fundamentalists and New Agers, and every other shade and color of spiritual bent humanity has been able to come up with over the past 5,000 years or so,
each held a single puzzle piece,
and without every single one of us
being willing to sit down together,
and being willing to put our puzzle piece on the table,
we could never discover
the answers to humanities survival on this planet as we have known it?

What if . . . the answers to our survival were entrusted to us collectively by the Divine to ensure
that either all will survive, or none will survive?
For we are all.....each and every one, children of the Most High God, and all beloved, cherished and irreplaceable in God's sight.

What if . . . each of us is a cell in the body of God,
and that by killing, maiming, starving,
or even threatening you in any way
I also threaten myself, since
the same Life-Force that flows through you
also flows through me,
and that by staunching its flow through you

I ALSO CUT OFF MY OWN SUPPLY?

What if . . . without your piece of the puzzle, your chant, your prayer wheel, your icon, your sacred dance, or ritual, my child's life could not be saved?

What if . . . without my willingness to invite my enemy—the Arab, Jew, Scientologist or Pagan to pray, dance, sing, or lay hands on my child, or children—all would perish?

Would my pride, my stubbornness, my self-righteousness be so unbending as to watch my own Children—the beloved of my heart, brought forth from my own flesh and blood—to perish because of my refusal to bend my knee and humble myself to beg for your help?

How many Mothers and Fathers are begging on bended knees today for sustenance, the barest of existence

> *"God does not call the qualified, God qualifies the called."*
> — Neale Donald Walsch, *Tomorrow's God*

for their offspring—the beloveds of their hearts—and we who have so much, who waste so much, overuse so much, and plow under so much, could end their suffering and death TODAY if we but chose to do so, do not hear, or hearing do not answer?

What if . . . all the killing stopped...suddenly...overnight, wouldn't we overpopulate the world? Wouldn't the overwhelming hordes of people be pushed off the continents into the oceans by the sheer mass of humanity?

Not perhaps if the cessation was a conscious choice—a deliberate decision, even if made only by what is called the "critical mass"—a shift in consciousness so dramatic that it could not arrive at a level of perception alone, but would be accompanied by at least the beginning awareness of what it would take to sustain life on earth—based on an enlightened understanding of the needs of Mother Earth and a paradigm shift toward *cooperation* and away from *competition* in every area of our lives.

WHAT IF?

Looking Toward Tomorrow: The Individual.
What Does It Mean To ME?

What if . . . you could be totally, 100% free—in body, mind and spirit?
How would you be different?
What would you be doing differently today if
you had been born in the right family?
Was born in the right body?
had gone to the right schools?
gotten the right education?
made all the right career choices?
had no disabilities of any kind:
mental, physical, or emotional?

What if . . . money had never been a problem?

What if . . . you had all the right connections?
knew all the right people?
lived in the right town?
had never been abused: mentally, emotionally, or physically?
had never had your spirit broken by society, teachers, family, or friends?

What if . . . you remembered who you really are?
Where you came from, and
Why you are here?

What if . . . you never learned to stay small so that others around you would be more comfortable?

What if . . . we were more interested in others' well-being than in our own?

What if . . . there was no war, famine, drought, or pestilence?

What if . . . we all lived together in peace, love, and joy?

What if . . . cooperation replaced competition?

What if . . . everyone was right and no one was wrong?

What if . . . everyone knew what you knew?

WHAT IF?

What amazing things could we accomplish together if all our combined energies were focused on solving the problems of the world regardless of who got the credit?

What if . . . we played nice and shared?

What if . . . we ate and drank only those things that blessed our bodies?

What if . . . we worked physically, using our bodies daily, so that exercise and the resulting well-being were natural to all?

What if . . . we recognized the divine inherent in ourselves, and each other?

What if . . . we could heal each other and ourselves naturally and energetically?

What if . . . we all died naturally—healthy and happy in our sleep?

What if . . . anyone who temporarily forgot who they were, and began to act in the old way were loved back, sung and danced back to wholeness by their community?

What if . . . *everything I did to YOU,*
I also experienced SIMULTANEOUSLY in myself?
How would I behave, think, and act differently?

What if . . . even 10% of these "What ifs" were true?

How would we change?
How would the world change?
How would humanity evolve and change?

What if . . . we really did know our Life's Purpose, our reason for coming to planet earth?

What if . . . we were not afraid to follow and fulfill it?

What if . . . we understood that everyone had a Life's Purpose to fulfill, and that it had nothing to do with money or things?

What if . . . our passion, our drive, our intention were focused on fulfilling our Purpose instead of accumulating more things?

What if . . . we could see with the eyes of God?

What if . . . we could see the BIG PICTURE, understand the long-term effects of our actions today, and have the opportunity to change those actions voluntarily, before it's too late?

What if . . . we cared so deeply about starving children that we were driven to come together in a world conference that did not end until a viable solution was reached by consensus?

What if . . . we found greater joy in living simply, needing less and wasting less?

What if . . . we went back to using the natural healing plants and herbs provided for us by God, instead of filling our bodies with drugs, which often cause more complications?

What if . . . doctors were paid to keep their patients healthy, and not paid if they became ill?

What if . . . hospitals became Healthy Living Centers where all were taught how to keep these magnificent instruments in tune, balance, and harmony: body, mind, and spirit?

What if . . . those small isolated schools—where radical change and total commitment has successfully educated all children regardless of race, faith, or economic status—became the most sought after models and therefore the norm for our entire educational system?

What if . . . parents and teachers begged for, demanded, and implemented these changes?

What if . . . it took only one person's commitment to make all of these 'What ifs' come true, and

What if . . . that person was YOU?

What if . . . you said "YES"?

What if . . . you said "NO"?

Let someone else do it, not me! I don't know enough, not smart enough, clever enough, or strong enough. They'll crucify me! No I can't. I'm too afraid I'll fail, and if I did succeed, it would change me too much. I wouldn't know who I was.

What if . . . no one else says YES?

What if . . . everyone in the world says:

> *Not me, not now, not that, let someone else do it.*
> *It's too hard, too scary, too dangerous?*

BUT . . .

What if . . . one person—a simple person—not a special person,

but an honest, kind and loving person stepped forward and said,
"I will do it. I will commit myself to believing that all
of this is possible,
to loving others more than myself,
to knowing my Life's Purpose and endeavoring to fulfill
it every day,
to seeing with the eyes of God,
to honoring the divine in you as well as in myself,
to being used by God for something greater than myself
every day,
to be humble, knowing that it is the Higher Power within me that
does the work,
to free myself from the need to get more, in order to feel like I am
finally enough,
to honor your faith tradition and to seek honestly to learn about
its teachings from you,
to walk softly upon the earth, taking only what I need, and sharing any overabundance with you."

What if . . . everyone on the planet said, YES

What if . . . everyone committed to living his or her life differently from this moment on?

HOW WOULD THE WORLD CHANGE?

HOW WOULD YOU CHANGE?

ACTION STEPS/YOUR TURN

Set some time aside when you will not be disturbed. (That is the challenge, isn't it?) Get quiet, let your breath become the pathway to your heart, and move into that sacred space, asking for ideas to flow through you, out and onto the page. Then just let go, read the questions, and jot down anything that comes to mind. It is all good. There are no wrong answers.

In an ideal world, how would you picture, imagine or envision, the following?

Let yourself dream the Big Dream! Just make it up.

1 How would our educational system change? What would it look like, sound like, feel like?

2 Our communities: Where and how would we live together differently?

3 Employment: How, where, and why would we work together, and for what purpose?

4 Finances: How would our needs be met? How would we be compensated for contributing our talents and abilities for the good of the whole?

5 Our primary relationships: How might they be transformed to be more cohesive, productive, and supportive of the best that is in each of us?

6 Third World Countries: How might they be brought into the world market? How might they become First World Countries in our lifetime?

7 Warring nations: How might we be able to see the world through their eyes and thus be able to see and seek viable solutions together?

8 If everyone in the world said "Yes," how could we come together to implement the possible solutions we envisioned collectively?

9 What part do you play in all of this? What is your role? What is your soul calling you to do, and what are you willing to commit to today?

Over the next week, contemplate these questions deeply during your quiet time. When you have an idea, a suggestion, or an inkling of an area in which you might be able to make a personal contribution to the healing of the planet and the survival of humanity, write it out in one short, simple, paragraph. Then date and sign it, thus creating a sacred contract with God. Read it every morning and night, and let its contents sink deeply into your subconscious mind. Understand that you do not have to know how to do what comes through you. All you have to do is commit to it.

10 Be alert to new opportunities that may come from totally unexpected directions. Be aware that they will probably not look anything like what you anticipated.

11 If an opportunity is presented and you're not certain that it's right for you, if you don't get that physical "hit"' that says "this is it," try saying, "Let me think about it and get back to you," rather than saying yes or no too quickly—then take it into your quiet time and the answer will come.

12 Record even the smallest actions you take which are in alignment with your Sacred Contract. You might invite a new acquaintance that is down on their luck to share a meal with you. You could visit a religious service unlike your own and perhaps take an introductory class. You could find a pen pal through the Internet in an oppressed country and create an ongoing dialogue in an endeavor to begin to understand the challenges they face in their daily life, and to offer encouragement and support. If you are sincere in your desire to participate consciously in the coming quantum leap humanity—including you—is about to take, you will know what is yours to do...and so will I.

The question remains:

Are you willing?

Am I?

Are we?

What if . . ?

Rule 1

It All Begins in the Mind!
There is no other way!

To be able to think a thought, be inspired by a new idea, make a decision to bring it about, and then

> *"You must do the thing you think you cannot do."*
> —Eleanor Roosevelt

see it become real right before your eyes—in spite of everything that said it couldn't be done—seems like a miracle, yet I have experienced such "miracles" in my own life over and over again; and you have, too.

Henry Ford said, "Whether you believe you can, or whether you believe you can't, you're right." As often as I have believed "I can," I have also believed "I can't," and I have proven my beliefs to be right both ways. Ford caught a vision of the mystery and the power of using our minds to create inner pictures of things that had never been, and held to that vision without wavering, as though it were already an accomplished fact, until it became a reality in his experience. Long before automobile piston-driven engines, as we know them, were invented, Ford saw the possibility in his mind, as though it were already an accomplished fact. He gave his engineers one year to come up with a prototype, but they said it was impossible.

Have you ever been told your dream was impossible? Did you then give it up, leaving an aching hole in your heart that you revisit on cold, rainy evenings; or did you, like Henry, hold to that vision with the tenacity of a bulldog while all the world called you a fool, only to reap the sweetest reward of all—to see the pictures in your mind, your dream, your vision, become a living, breathing reality in your world? There is nothing to compare with the experience of knowing that there is an unlimited creative power in the Universe that is available to you and that, together, you can bring about that which has never been done before. In fact, that is how everything we take for granted today came into being; someone, somewhere, had a thought, dreamed a dream, and their dream became so real for them it would not let them go. It's true, too, that some inventions have been the results of so-called "accidents," but the individuals who discovered them were intensely engrossed in bringing another idea into being, which created an opening for this perhaps even better idea to take form through them.

It All Begins in The Mind!
There is no other way!

We tend to think that others are just "lucky," or have all the breaks, while we have none, but creative people make their breaks and are ready when lady luck comes around. They expect to be successful. Somewhere down deep in their hearts, their dreams would not let them go. Each time Ford checked on the progress of his design team and they told him in exasperation that it couldn't be done, he would answer something like, "Oh, yes it can—and it will. Keep on working."

Affirmations are positive, present tense statements that speak of our vision, our dream as if it were an already accomplished fact. Creating and repeating our affirmations allows us to reprogram our beliefs and the beliefs of others from "it's impossible, it can't be done" to "oh, yes it can, and it will," and gives us the energy, drive, and focus to "keep working." The purpose of writing and speaking our affirmations is to convince our own mind that it is possible and doable and that we can do it.

In creating affirmations, we use the most powerful, positive wording we can possibly arrive at, so that we can actually feel the truth of it resonate in our bodies—that gut feeling. It is as if our very bones feel the ring of truth in our affirmative statement and respond with a delightful little shout of, "Yes, oh, yes!"

So, in creating an affirmation for Rule #1, I might reason aloud something like this: Since everything begins in mind, and since everything I see and use in my world was first an idea in someone's mind, and since I, too, have a mind and have brought my ideas into reality over and over without realizing I was doing it, I can now choose to do it consciously. My affirmation then might look something like this.

I now choose to cooperate consciously with the Universal Power that uses the ideas I create in my mind, along with my unshakeable belief that it can be done, to unfailingly bringing it about.

It is as if our ideas create pictures in our mind, which form a negative image on a strip of film, which at first cannot be seen. Before digital pictures and Polaroids, the image on the negative would be impressed on photographic paper by focusing an intensive beam of light through the negative onto the paper, but the sheet receiving the image still appeared to be blank until submerged in a special chemical solution, which caused the image to slowly appear as if by magic. If the paper receiving the image were not held in the chemical solution long enough for the picture to develop, a partial picture might emerge, unclear, fuzzy, or with parts missing. That is why it is important for us to impress the image of our desire clearly in Universal Mind by repeating it daily, until we see it "develop" in our physical experience.

Action Steps/Your Turn

1 Create an affirmation for yourself. Choose something measurable rather than abstract, so that you will have physical proof when your affirmation creates your chosen reality. Example: If you say you want to be healthier, how healthy is healthy enough? However, if you say you choose to exercise three times a week in order to live in a healthier body, you will know when you have accomplished it.

2 Keep it short and simple; one sentence that clearly states your desired result.

3 Try different word combinations until you feel it in your body! You will get a "hit," a felt sense when you are on target.

4 Set it aside and come back later. Read it aloud and be willing to change it until it feels right, until it rings true.

5 Don't stress over it or try too hard. Relax and have fun with it. Treat it as an experiment.

6 Remember, the Universal Power is Limitless, so don't be afraid to think big!

Rule 2

Ask For What You Really Want. Do not settle for what you think you can have.

The wisdom of the ages teaches that we have two minds. One is our logical, reasoning mind, the one we are most familiar with, the one we use every day. We use this mind, which I will call the "Thinker," to decide

> *"...through it all, there is the one—ageless, knowing, responding to our upraised consciousness. It is always itself as we discover it over and over for the first time."*
> – Dr. Margaret Stortz

whether to have a hamburger or fish tacos, go to school or ditch, stay in a job we hate or leave, pay our fair share of taxes or cheat. It reasons things out and makes decisions based on the available information, and especially on past experiences, our history.

Each time we approach a new experience, we tend to see it through the lens of these past experiences. For instance, if you have had several failed love relationships, or business or financial ventures, you may approach the next blind date, stock option, or business opportunity with less enthusiasm, commitment, or expectation of success. Everything is energy and without a total commitment of our energy on any venture, its possibilities for success are limited. However, if you have been "lucky in love" or if "everything you touch turns to gold," you may tend to enter any new adventure with a much greater commitment of energy

and enthusiasm, thus fueling the venture with a greater possibility for success.

People love to be around successful people because they give
off an aura of such self-confidence even though they may not say
a word. When my husband and I did the EST training in the '70s,
everyone assumed he was a producer because he had a deep sense
of who he was and had no need to try to convince anyone that he
was okay. He knew it, and that was enough. That brings us to our
second mind, which I will call the "Knower." They are actually
both just different ways of using the One Mind.

The Knower makes decisions, but not based on information
gathered by our five senses or on our past experiences. Rather, it
taps into the energy of the One Mind, the Intelligent Energy that
runs the whole Universe, the inherent wisdom in Nature that
causes the seasons to come and go, tides to rise and fall, and the
planets to spin on their individual trajectories.

We all play a better game when we know the rules. All games
have rules, but the rules of the Game of Life are not written
down, or they are hidden in mystery or metaphor in the sacred
books of the ages. These "Rules" flow out of the "Lessons" I have
proven in my own life, often painfully, but which I have found
always lead me to joy when I remember to follow them. Since life
is a process and not a destination, I am still learning; this is just the
beginning, and more will follow as I discover and prove them in
my own life.

When we have seen something to be, or to function in the same
way for some time and it changes, we either can't see the change
or we resist it with every bone in our bodies, because it goes
against our established set of "Rules" regarding that thing, that
our Thinker believes keeps us safe in the world. When someone

changes the rules in the middle of the game without our permission, the Thinker feels out of control (which is a hallucination anyway) and hits the panic button. The structure of our individual Game of Life, the rules we have created and agreed to play by, are being pulled out from under us; our very world is being shaken to the core, and we may feel terrified.

Because our very life depended on being fed and cared for as an infant, being abandoned, neglected, or abused caused tremendous fear in us, the very

"What we play is life."
– Louis Armstrong

real fear of death. The infant's fears for survival at the time were valid, but those memories of fear, abandonment, and survival are buried deep in our subconscious and rear their frightened heads when our world is shaken by unexpected changes. It is reasonable to experience fear, abandonment, and loss—even the fear of survival at the death of a loved one, or a terminal diagnosis, but it is not reasonable to experience these same fears when we want to ask our boss for a raise or change careers—yet experience them we may.

Long before I learned these Rules of the Game and understood that it was the thoughts in my own mind that determined my destiny and not any authority figure sitting behind any desk anywhere, it was next to impossible for me to ask for what I wanted, or to express an opposing viewpoint, idea, or suggestion. Unrealistic, baseless fears that felt like the infant in me was going to die would clamp my throat shut so that the words (which my infant apparently believed would seal my doom) could not be spoken. I remember now with great chagrin sitting in the office of my high-powered boss in her high-powered agency on the corner of Hollywood Boulevard and Highland, frozen solid, bawling my eyes out and unable to communicate why I was so unhappy, unable to say what was on my mind, while she played twenty questions, trying to figure out who the heck was dying! Actually, it felt like I was dying inside, but what was really happening was that I was beginning to rewrite the Rules of my own Game. My new rule regarding asking for what I want is:

I Ask for What I Really Want, and Do Not Settle for What I THINK I Can Have!

At the end of a class on prosperity and abundance that I recently took, the facilitator said she had a gift for us, a token to remember our experience. She held a basket high and asked us to reach in and take one. When it was my turn, I did as directed, only to discover a moment later that the new dollar bills on which she had written words like Abundance, Joy, Harmony, etc. had stuck together and I had two. Embarrassed that I had "made a mistake," and because my ego always strives to look good, I quickly started to put one back, but Rev. Harmony said that it was mine, that it came to me because I am abundant, and that I must keep it.

This little scenario showed me:

a. How quick I am to give back the greater good the Universe wants to give me, to deny myself the fruits of my work in mind and heart to establish an abundant consciousness.
b. The extra dollar I tried to give back, but which is now mine, had the word ABUNDANCE written on it in red ink!

I do not settle for the little my Thinker THINKS I can have.

These sneaky little fear thoughts try to keep us small, invisible, and safe, but there is a part of me that is bigger than life, out there, risking on the skinny branches, and when I am listening to that voice (my other mind, the Knower), I am most alive!

ACTION STEPS/YOUR TURN

1 When do you feel most alive? Write the first three things that come to mind. Don't worry if it doesn't make any sense, given your present circumstances.

_____

_____

_____

2 When do you feel most out of control? What, if anything, pushes your panic buttons? Jot down a word or two that identifies these situations for you.

_____

_____

_____

3 What unwritten "Rules" might you have been unaware of that trigger the above, and how could you change them for the better?

_____

_____

_____

4 Remember a time when you did not give in to please another; when you asked for what you really wanted and did not
settle for what you thought you could have.
☙

_____

_____

_____

_____

_____

_____

5 What could you do to spend more time doing the things that
make you feel most alive?
☙

_____

_____

_____

_____

_____

_____

Rule 3

You don't have to know how to do a thing in order to do it. Just Trust and Begin.

The power we are using is the same Universal Power that operates our whole universe, effortlessly. We sometimes call it Mother Nature. We marvel at the

> *"To find our calling is to find the intersection between our own deep gladness and the world's deep hunger."*
> — Frederick Buechner

miracle of birth, are stunned by the shattering beauty of a sunset on the ocean, or a symphony that moves us to tears.

As you are reading this book, this power I speak of is digesting your food, growing your hair, and replacing your bones: at the same time, it spins the planet you are riding on, while providing you with the proper quality and quantity of air, food, and water you need to sustain life as you know it here on earth. Of course, it is also doing the same thing for every single living thing everywhere, not only here but also throughout the universe all at the same time, which is why we say it is limitless! Awesome!

On day three of my experience of writing this book, I need to tell you that I honestly do not know how to do it. I have never written a book before, but then I had never written and performed a one-woman show before either, but the limitless Universal Power created it magnificently through me (but that is another story!). In fact, I had begun another book, which I felt "destined" to write, but my second mind, my inner Knower, showed me clearly that this is the book I am to write now, and that I am also to create a Web site with the same name. In fact, I got the Web site name first, which is how I understood that this was the work I was to do now.

Therefore, as I begin, I do not know what it is to be about; I do not have an outline, nor was I hit by a bolt of lightning in which I "saw" the whole thing complete. However, having had years of experience in which this invisible Power has proven over and over again to my utter amazement that if I will just trust it and begin, it can perform what seems like miracles through me.

I remember a summer conference in which the facilitator, Dr. Kathy Hearn, was teaching about meditation. She said the way to begin was to "get your seat in the seat," in other words, to show up. Therefore, with a project I am committed to completing, and with no idea whatsoever how to begin, I made a solemn commitment to

"If the heart wills, the hand gathers the fingers to write a book."
– Rumi

"get my seat in the seat," to simply show up and start. What that looks like is rising an hour earlier than usual (I'm still working on that!) and sitting down with my pad and pen and opening myself in loving trust to that Infinite Knower that knows how to work through me to make it all happen.

What Its process is I cannot tell you. I can only tell you that it works when I trust It utterly and completely and throw myself open to Its limitless creativity. It is stunning to be on the receiving end of such a process and to be the conduit for something new to come into the world.

It is crucially important for you to understand that I cannot do this with my Thinker, with my logical, reasoning mind, because it already knows it does not know how to do it. Therefore, I must set it aside and surrender to the Greater Power that does know. It is like the blind man in the Bible who was healed by Jesus and was trying his best to answer the questions put to him by the Pharisees regarding this miraculous healing and the man, Jesus, who brought it about. Finally, and probably in great exasperation at his inability to explain it rationally, he said, "...One thing I do know. I was blind but now I see." (John 9:25, New International Version)

Therefore, the "proof of the pudding" will be somewhere down the line on page 75, 150, or whatever, when this amazing experience is complete and I am holding this book in my hands. However, it is not about being an "author" and all that might seem to imply; it is much more about experiencing the process of creation, of being that conduit I spoke of, and about learning to trust it. What I have learned—often the hard way through trial and error—is that when I started to listen to those inner "hunches, gut feelings, or intuitions" (which are some of the ways our inner Knower communicates with us), and trusted them enough to follow them in the little things, I gained confidence and was willing to trust them in the bigger things as well.

ACTION STEPS/YOUR TURN

1 Remember a time when you listened to your inner Knower, when you followed your "hunch, intuition, or gut instinct." Write briefly about the outcome.

ᴄᴏ

_____

_____

_____

_____

_____

_____

2 Were you aware at the time that you had been guided by a Power greater than you are? If so, try to recall the feeling when you realized that you were not alone.

ᴄᴏ

_____

_____

_____

_____

_____

3 Remember a time when you ignored your "gut instinct." Write briefly about the outcome.

 ☞

_____

_____

_____

_____

_____

_____

4 Recall, if you can, the feeling when you realized that you had received guidance, but did not trust it.

 ☞

_____

_____

_____

_____

_____

_____

Make a commitment to listening to your intuition, to trust it and to follow its guidance, as you understand it to be.

Rule 4

Fear Repels/ Love Attracts.
That which we struggle to get, grab,
or hang onto, we push away.
That which we trust, release, and
invite, we draw to us.

I moved into a townhouse last weekend and brought my beloved kitty companion, Spirit, with me. I was warned by my neighbors that several

"There is nothing to fear but fear itself."
—Franklin Delano Roosevelt

kitty friends had been eaten by coyotes on our property and that I should not let her out, *especially at night.* Well, of course, she got out last night and although several passers-by offered their assistance, we were unable to catch her. The harder we tried, the faster she flew to escape our closing trap. I finally decided to sit quietly on a step nearby and enjoy the cool night air and all the new sights, sounds, and smells that must have been so deliciously exciting to her kitty senses. I told her I loved her and that I wanted her to be safe and that I would leave the door open for her when she was ready so that she could find her way home amidst our huge complex.

Any animal lover will understand my Thinker's fear for her safety; however, my Knower told me that our collective fears were causing her to run away instead of coming to me. I chose consciously to trust the guidance within her (as she is a part of Nature, so she is guided just as the stars and planets are guided) that would bring her home safely or take her on another path and told myself that it was out of my hands. I surrendered to the Higher Power within us both, went inside, propped the door open, and became totally engrossed in some pictures in a box in the garage of my recently departed husband and I on our trip through Europe a few years ago. I completely let go of my desire, *my* need to get *my* cat in *my* house on *my* timetable! That's called control!

When I had finished reminiscing about the joys we shared touring through Europe, I went out front, heard Spirit meow, called her, and she immediately came into the house. That is a miracle because she had never before come when I called, and with tears running down my face, I gave deep and humble thanks for her safe return.

It's hard to let go when every cell in our bodies is tied up in knots and our Thinker is screaming:

NO!!! STOP!

I CAN'T GO THERE!

IT'S TOO HIGH!

IT'S TOO HARD!

IT'S TOO SCARY!

But when we can learn to trust the quiet voice within that assures us that all will be well when we just let go, all those scary thoughts seem to lose their power, to melt away, and an indescribable peace takes their place.

Action Steps/Your Turn

1 Write about a time when, in spite of your fear-driven need to control (to make something come out your way), you listened to a different voice and trusted it enough to follow it. See if you can identify the feeling that replaced the fear when you made that decision.

ᢙᡃ

_____

_____

_____

_____

2 Remember a time when your fear-driven needs were in total control, leaving you to struggle to get, grab, or hang on to something or someone. Briefly jot down the outcome and compare the feelings you experienced when following these two very different paths.

ᢙᡃ

_____

_____

_____

_____

_____

_____

Rule 5

Love: The Power Behind It All—
The central core of the universe...
The glue that holds it together.

That which is mine comes to me naturally and effortlessly, as if drawn by an invisible magnet, when the expectation of my heart is open wide in gratitude and joy at being the recipient of

"Love resounds through you, almost shattering the vessel containing it, and spills back out into the world, delighting all of those in your sphere."
—Rev. Nancy Zala

the good gifts of the Universe. Understand that I am speaking here of being grateful for that which I cannot see or hold in my hand, yet I can trust that this greater good is on its way to me. I do not even know its name or what it looks like, but I know it will bless others and me—through me—in some way I cannot at this moment comprehend.

Nevertheless, I can appreciate and give thanks for the miracle of creation that is going on continually through me, through you, and through everyone, everywhere!

The energy of this Universal Power is Love. The activity of Love is to give—to give of Itself, wholly, continuously, and without limits. Love is not a miser, does not hoard Itself, nor save some of Itself for a rainy day. Love gives because it is Its nature to give. That is why we are in such ecstasy when we are truly, freely giving our love.

A static love is no love at all. The kind of love I am speaking of here is a verb, an action word and without the activity of giving Itself away, it exists for us only in a dream state as a remote possibility, or perhaps something we observe in other people, but not as a part of our own life experience. It requires a deep surrender, an abandonment of the fears and defenses of our Thinker, whose job (it believes) is to keep us safe at all costs, to throw ourselves into Love's arms, expecting nothing in return. The world teaches that we need to get our fair share and that if we don't fight for it, someone else will get what is ours, but that is not Love's way.

> *The flowers bloom and open themselves*
> *to the sun's warmth out of love.*
> *Great music, art, and literature pour from*
> *the hearts of their authors with love.*
> *The hand that holds this pen is moved upon by*
> *a heart overflowing with love.*
> *And when tears flow from our eyes at a phrase,*
> *a melody, a poem, or a flower,*
> *It is because the love in our hearts has been touched by the*
> *Great Love of the Creator of all things*
> *who brought its beauty into being.*

Some months before my father died, my cousin, who is like a sister to me, sat on his bed and poured out her love. She told him that he was her hero, and that he had provided a role model for her life. She said it was important to her that he know how much he meant to her, and that she was not willing to take a chance on being unable to say it while he was still with us.

We tend to take our loved ones for granted, especially if we have been together for many years. But they cannot read our minds, so it is up to us to tell them simply and clearly how we feel

ACTION STEPS/YOUR TURN

1 Write a love letter to your beloved. If you have never done it before, there is no better time to start than now.

2 Go to the library and check out a book of poetry on love, perhaps something by Elizabeth Barrett Browning. Keep it by your bed, and read a page or two each night just before going to sleep. Let the words, and the feelings that generated them, reach across time and touch the part of you that loves.

3 When you are ready to set pen to paper, or sit at your computer, open your heart and let those things you have always felt and wanted to say flow out onto the page.

4 Do not edit your letter, especially not while you are writing it. Just let it all pour out, until you feel complete.

5 Set it aside for a day or so, then take it out and reread it. Any changes can easily be made, but remember that your first thoughts are usually on target, so if possible, send it off just like it is.

6 Mail it rather than delivering it in person. Allow the recipient to feel genuine surprise and delight at your efforts to express in perhaps a new and more deeply honest and forthright way, your truest feelings for them.

7 If you are experiencing difficulties in your relationship, if communications have been strained, or even cut off, you may not feel loving just now. Write it anyway. Even if you do not mail it, it will remind you of all the things you loved about them in the beginning and perhaps provide an opening for further dialogue and eventual healing.

Healing does not always mean getting back together. Sometimes it means going your separate ways, but even separation can be done with love. If you are both willing to look honestly at the cause of the breakup, you can both leave healed and whole, blessing the time you had together, choosing to remember the good times you shared, and releasing anything that does not give you joy.

Resentment Kills.

Since this energy of Love is what fuels our very life force, to deliberately withhold this love as a form of punishment is to operate against the power of the Universe and, as such, is an unconscious death wish.

Rule

W hat dies are not necessarily our bodies, although they most certainly can be affected. This kind of death operates on a more subtle field: the field of our

"Love yourself, forgive yourself for the feelings you may have harbored, or still have."
—Rev. Nancy Zala

dreams, our hopes, our energy, our creativity. Since we were not aware of this most basic Rule of the Game of Life, we tend to look outside ourselves to find someone or something to blame for our loss. Taking responsibility for the consequences of our actions allows us to take back our power. It is not at all a matter of blame or guilt; it is, instead, the doorway to freedom.

My mother was one of the most deeply spiritual, loving, and giving people I have ever known, but those qualities, for which she was so loved, respected, and admired did not come cheaply. She paid for them dearly. In the early years of my parents' marriage, during the depression, she was forced to have abortions. The facts seemed simple; they could not afford another mouth to feed (they already had my brother, Jim). My father's duty, as he saw it at the time, was to raise the enormous sum of $50, while Mother took the streetcar alone to tear the child conceived with love from her womb and from her heart. Though she understood the facts, the emotional and psychological wounds went deep and perhaps formed scar tissue upon her loving nature.

It is impossible for us today, who enjoy such a level of affluence (and who are protected by so many safety nets should that affluence ever disappear), to try to understand the lives our parents and grandparents lived when there were no such safety nets in place. There was no work to be found and nowhere to go for financial aid, food, or medical care, so people went hungry and feared for the very survival of their families and their children. That explains why my father's guaranteed income of $98.00 a month as a Seaman 1st Class in the U.S. Navy was such a godsend. With it, he helped support his brother's family as well as other friends in need. These were the harsh realities they faced that required making such heart-rending decisions.

I recall my mother-in-law, a very pragmatic, bright, and generous woman saying that she could not remember one single young woman friend that did not have at least one abortion during the desperate years of the depression. However, the memory that really brought it home to me was when she told us that she was the only child in her school who could not donate at least 25-cents to some noble cause during the year, therefore sat on the steps of the school all day while the rest of her schoolmates went on a field trip (a fact she never told her mother because, even at her tender young age, she understood that there was nothing her mother could have done about it). It was during this time and under these horrific circumstances that my parents, and so many others, did what had to be done, though it tore them apart inside.

We were living in Pearl Harbor when the bombs began to fall on December 7, 1941, and while Mother, Jim, and I were evacuated, Daddy stayed behind and did not come home to stay until the war was over in 1945. During those years, his world expanded enormously. He had become a world traveler, dined with admirals, commanded hundreds of men, and looked death in the face. At the same time, Mother had withdrawn from the world, venturing out only to visit family, and had thrown herself into her spiritual studies. Living daily with the fear that he might never return, she found a faith she could cling to for strength and support. When he finally came home, they discovered that they had grown apart, and the adjustment period was difficult, as it is for all returning combat veterans and their spouses.

I was thirteen years old when she became pregnant, and I was deliriously happy at the prospect of having a new baby sister or brother and began my childish attempts at knitting little baby things. Looking back now, I can see how all the unresolved pain from the past caused my Mother's loving heart to begin to shut down.

She grew cold and distant to my father, who idolized her, and who, I am sure, had no idea what was causing her such unhappiness (nor, I believe, did she). Remember that women in their late thirties did not give birth in the 1940s, and she was embarrassed, resentful, and deeply enraged. She refused to speak to him for days on end except as a necessity. Even the anticipation of holding the infant her heart had ached for so many years before could not bring her happiness. She stubbornly refused to see the good and instead, became mired in blame and resentment, and the joy within her died.

When my baby sister was to be born, Mother chose a Christian Science nursing center many miles from our home, shutting my father out even more completely. Because he did not understand her new spiritual path, or how she had changed in his absence, he could not bring himself to participate in the process. Perhaps the experience of sending her alone on the streetcar for the abortions when they were both so young was what caused him to drop her off when she went into labor. When he saw that she was well taken care of, he bundled his broken-hearted daughter back into the car to take me home, leaving my Mother alone once again. When the phone rang in the middle of the night telling us that my baby sister had died during birth, and that the umbilical cord had wrapped around her throat, squeezing the life out of her, my happy, childlike world came tumbling down. Before Mother came home, I packed away all the baby things we had made and had the bassinet we covered together taken away.

It was many, many years later, when I had children of my own, and when both of us had found a new spiritual path that brought us joy, great love, and freedom, that my mother shared with me the greatest lesson of her life, and the one that my baby sister brought during her briefest of sojourns on earth. It was this:

"Resentment kills."

My children and my children's children never knew the cold, silent, hurting woman my mother was before she understood the blessing this experience was to her. She loved my father unconditionally, as she always had, as she did all of us. She gave generously of herself and her love and was ever-ready to lend a helping hand whenever and wherever needed. She and my father had the most beautiful, loving relationship it has ever been my privilege to witness.

All our attempts to get our own way, prove we are right, and therefore someone else is wrong; or withhold our love as a secret punishment for real or imagined wrongs—will lead to our downfall. Misusing the Power of Love in this way squeezes the joy out of life and leaves it empty and arid, without the Life Energy required to bring forth new life, new ideas, or our dreams into reality. It robs us of our spontaneity, enthusiasm, and playfulness—which are the fertile ground of creativity—and makes us old before our time.

"Forgiveness means giving up all hope for a better past."
– **William Paul Hansen**, *Hope Heals*

As my mother took responsibility for the consequences of her actions, she took back her power and set herself free to live and love fully once again. Her life, their life together, was rich beyond measure. My parents were deeply loved, respected, and admired by all. Both of them lived happy, active, healthy lives until they were almost ninety!

ACTION STEPS/YOUR TURN

1 With your journal in hand, sit quietly with this idea: Take three deep breaths, and then shift your focus from your head to your heart center where wisdom dwells. Gently allow yourself to revisit those times you have withheld your love, and simply notice what may have died: your dream, your relationship, an opportunity for advancement, success, your aliveness, your joy?

2 Allow your thoughts to pour out into your journal. They are only thoughts, and no matter how painful, they cannot hurt you. Know that this is an important breakthrough for you and give yourself all the time you need. Write until you feel spent, until you feel empty.

3 Write a letter to Life about your discoveries and about what you have learned.

4 Write a second letter from Life back to you filled with reassurance that Love has never been truly withdrawn from you and that your choices simply limited your experience of its fullness in your life. Put everything you ever wanted to hear regarding your talents and abilities, and the special gifts you bring to the world, into this letter. Give yourself all the love you so deeply desire. Be lavish, but be true.

5 Write a thank you note back to Life. Include in it the new choices you are making based on your new understanding.

Rule 7

Bind Another/Bind Yourself.
Free Another/Free Yourself.

The rope we use to keep our secret hostages in bondage is woven out of our own Life Energy; therefore, every time we tighten the rope, which we imagine will make them suffer, we are strangling our own life!

"Search out the unhealed wounds, the familiar patterns of betrayal and injustice. Look courageously at each one and you will see it become a doorway to greater peace and joy."
—Joanne Blum, *On Edge: From Discomfort to Discovery*

Your willingness to let go creates a chink in the armor of your defenses that allows the love in your heart to shine through and the power of Love does the rest.

As a spiritual counselor, I have heard horror stories from those who were unable to defend themselves at the time. While not denying the real physical and psychological pain involved, I still believe it is possible to free ourselves from the pain of the past. I believe it only because I have been privileged to witness the transformation that takes place in an individual when someone is willing to be willing. No matter how long or dark the tunnel—and not even daring to hope they could ever be free or whole again, but with no other way out—they somehow found the courage to begin, and in the process, got their lives back.

If this has been a part of your life experience, or of someone you love, be patient. The deeper the wound, the longer it takes to heal. In the world of medicine, it is important that the healing take place from the inside out. I got a nasty gash in my shin when I was a teenager; it sealed over before the deep healing took place and became infected. The doctor had to remove the surface scab so that the deep healing could occur.

We try to bury terrifying images of brutal, inhumane acts, but until they are faced and brought into the light with the compassionate guidance of a trained professional, they remain hidden, scabbed over, but spreading their poisonous infection ever deeper, eating away at the fabric of our lives—much like the wound in my leg.

Action Steps/Your Turn

1 Think of a time when you accepted your part in creating some difficult or painful experience instead of blaming the other person. Notice that when you set the other person free you were automatically set free as well. Remember, the feeling as your Life Energy was released in your own body through this activation of the power of Love.

2 When you go to bed tonight, ask your Higher Power to soften your heart, to make you willing to set yourself free by releasing anyone and everyone you may be holding in bondage. Is there someone you are holding in bondage right now: your boss or co-worker, your ex, your parents, or someone else? Imagine what it would feel like if, through your willingness to set them free, your Life Energy were doubled, or tripled, to accomplish all your dreams. Perhaps you've even forgotten what it feels like to be fully alive and enthusiastic about life. Consider the cost in terms of your Life Energy to continue to hold this person or persons in bondage. Ask yourself honestly if it is worth it. Just being *willing* is all that is required. Your willingness opens the door to the freedom you long for, and the love that you are will show the way.

3 Think of someone you deeply respect and admire, whose ways of being and living in the world created a model that helped mold the way you live your life. Write them a letter acknowledging the difference they made in your life, even if they are no longer living. If you cannot contact them directly, drop it in the postal mailbox with just their name on it, knowing that somehow they will get your message.

4   As a part of your counseling experience, you may be asked to write a letter to an individual who caused you unspeakable pain. Let all the rage, humiliation, resentment, and resistance pour out of your soul and onto the page. Remember, they are only words and words cannot hurt you. You will know it when the release comes because you will still remember the incident that caused you pain as a fact, but there will be no emotional charge attached to it. Be certain that you create a safe space for this activity where you will be uninterrupted. I am not a psychologist, nor would I presume to suggest that there is an easy answer to your pain. However, if you are harboring any dark secret of which you are terrified or ashamed, please consider seeking professional help. Try to imagine it as that infection in my leg, covered over and looking okay on the outside, but doing its poisonous work on the inside.

OUR DARKEST FEARS CANNOT SURVIVE
THE LIGHT OF DAY.

My mother had a spiritual practitioner when I was young who used to say, "Bring error into the light." (Error meaning evil, fear, or false beliefs.) That is why, as kids, all the "bogeymen" disappeared when the sun came up in the morning. It feels like time for a break, so here goes.

---

5 GET OUTSIDE! Take a walk in Nature, breathe in that delicious Breath of Life, smell a flower, lie in the grass, or count the stars. Forget about everything for a while. Notice how good it feels to be ALIVE and give thanks for one more day of life, one more opportunity to be a blessing, to make someone smile, to rock a baby, pet a dog, or sing a song. Life is good. It is a gift from the Universe and we don't want to waste a single minute of it. So while you're walking, or counting the stars, hum a little melody softly to yourself and see if it doesn't make your heart smile.

Rule 8

Gratitude is the Gateway, through which more blessings flow.

I learned this rule early in life at my mother's knee, although I did not understand or practice it well until much later in life.

As I write this morning, I am sitting on the deck of my

"In order to have what we want, we must want what we have. Gratitude for where we are and what we have is a powerful healing attitude."
—A Foundational Class student

new home looking out across a wide expanse of lush green grass and magnificent trees. The sun's light through the leaves creates ever-shifting patterns on the page as I write, and I am filled to overflowing with a deep sense of gratitude and joy. I live two blocks from a major freeway and just off a busy thoroughfare, yet here, in this tranquil oasis, I feel such serenity, such peace. The sounds of life's activities going on around me form a background symphony, which, rather than disturb, adds to the wonder of this amazing space.

No astute businessperson would ever build such a development today. They would tear down Nature's beauty and fill it with concrete and steel. That is why I bought this forty-year-old townhouse with the rusty sinks, moldy black shower pans, and doors that don't lock, instead of a much newer, spanking clean one across town whose acquiescence to our need for the beauty of

Nature was a ten by ten foot concrete pad next to the sidewalk of another busy street.

I am grateful I was led here, grateful for the dear couple who purchased my former home—allowing me the means with which to buy this one. I am grateful for the twelve years we lived in our beautiful home near the ocean, for all the friends I made there, and for those who showed up and dug in to help me make this move. I am grateful for my family, for our closeness, and for their readiness to show up whenever I have a need. I am grateful for the miracle of healing that took place in my body last year when I was in and out of the hospital for several months with a nasty case of pneumonia. I am grateful for the fifty years I had the privilege of sharing my life and my love with my husband, Dick. I am grateful for the guidance and wisdom of my inner Knower that is allowing me to reinvent myself as a newly single, widowed woman.

> *"...I have set before thee an open door and no man can shut it."*
> – (Revelations 3:8, King James Version)

Oh yes, there are days when I still weep bitter tears and feel sorry for myself, or feel overwhelmed with all the added responsibilities and decisions I am required to make as a single woman. Then, I marvel at all you single parents that struggle daily to be both mother and father—who provide not only food and shelter, but guidance, love, and a sense of security to their children—and I am humbled by your willingness to just show up for one more day, one more meal cooked, one more skinned knee to kiss and make better.

Action Steps/Your Turn

1 Write the things for which you are grateful. If times have been difficult and you have a hard time getting started, begin with your body and its abilities to laugh, run, see, think, hear, taste, and enjoy life.

2 If you find that you particularly enjoy this activity, or if you strongly resist it, set some time aside this week and write 100 or 1,000 things for which you are grateful. It can change your life! The harder it is to do, the greater will be your reward. So stick with it in spite of any resistance.

3 Create a Gratitude Journal. Begin every day by writing at least three things for which you are grateful. Looking for things for which to be grateful will open your eyes to how much you may have taken for granted.

4 Say "Thank you" more often, and mean it.

5 Call someone who is always there for you—your best friend, family member, or co-worker—and thank them. Share with them the difference they make in your life.

6 Each night, when you go to bed, and each morning, when you waken, thank your Higher Power for the blessings of that day—for simple things like clean sheets and a roof over your head, for food to eat and loved ones with whom to share your life.

No One Else Has Your Answers.
No counselor, psychologist, doctor,
spouse, or guru. Your answers lie
within you and mine within me.

Rule **9**

Working through a life problem;
a pattern for success.

L ife continually presents
us with variations on its
Rules to see if we really get
it, or if we are paying attention. Something is bugging
me and I decided to share it
with you. Sometimes in just
talking it out, we come to our own understanding.

> *"Courage allows the successful*
> *woman to fail—and to learn*
> *powerful lessons from the*
> *failure—so that in the end,*
> *she didn't fail at all."*
> — Maya Angelou

As a spiritual counselor, I have been trained to listen with one
ear to the client's concerns and the other to my inner Knower.
Guided by this inner wisdom, we move together to a deeper
realm of knowing, from our heads to our hearts, from problems
to solutions. Here, if they are willing, the answers they are seeking will reveal themselves, sometimes after many years of struggle, with astounding clarity and simplicity. The client often
believes that I, or another counselor, has performed some miracle, but the miracle lies in their willingness to—

1 Admit that there is a problem;
2 Ask humbly for help;
3 Accept responsibility for their part in creating it (nothing is
really healed without this crucial step); and

4   Be willing to hear the answer, even when it feels uncomfort able or scary.

Therefore, here is my problem. I am not happy with the color my kitchen was painted. I was not here when the painting was done (I was still in San Diego). In my unpacking, I recently discovered the sample of the color I chose and guess what: The kitchen was not painted with the color I ordered! It is close, but not what I ordered.

The contractor had called to tell me he was having difficulty getting the color I chose and that they did not sell it anymore. I said I had picked up a brochure just a few days before and gave him the name, brand, and color formula. Here is where I think I am stuck. If he had just called me and communicated that he still could not get the exact color I ordered, but that he was willing to do his best to match it, and asked if that was OK with me, I am sure I would have said yes, because I wanted the painting done before I moved in.

If I had expected a change, I would not have been surprised and disappointed when I walked in. Instead, I would have been grate-ful for the contractor's efforts to please me and for his willingness to be truthful, even at the risk of my displeasure.

Therefore, I guess it is really about not being asked, not being included in the decision-making rather than the color itself. (I think we may be getting somewhere.)

So let us go back to our Formula for Success.

1   The Problem: I am annoyed that I was not consulted regarding the change in the color I ordered for my kitchen to be painted.

2   Asking for Help: I am humbling myself by letting my Thinker/Controller spill its guts with you and in public, and by trusting this process to reveal my answer!

3 Accepting Responsibility: Perhaps I should have been here for such an important and costly event, or followed up by calling to make sure all was well. However, that is all in the past and cannot be changed! What is important is this: What are my options now, and what is my responsibility today?

4 Am I willing to hear the answer, even if it is my fault?

a I can continue to feel frustrated and annoyed every time I step into the kitchen (Yuk!); or

b I can accept that it's done, it's pretty (ho-hum), clean and fresh, and forget it (not likely); or

c I can call the contractor and communicate my frustration. (Oh, oh! This is where my Thinker's fear tends to rear its ugly head.)

Back to The Problem:

Now I do not think the color is the issue at all. I think the issue, instead, is the old recurring one in my life, that is, the inability to ask for what I really want and expect to get it.

Back to Rule #2:

Oftentimes, my Formula for misery and martyrdom in the past was to continue to suffer in silence rather than to face my fears and risk being rejected and/or unloved (boring!). Can anyone relate? Now Life has offered me another opportunity to take a risk, face my fears, and make a new choice. That is very different from being unhappy with the color. *This is an important shift in my awareness. Do not miss it!* You are going to apply it to yourself in the Action Step.

Back to Rule #2:

Am I willing to *ask for what I really want,* or will I dishonor my own needs and silence my "voice" yet again?

Understand that the contractor's response is relatively unimportant. What is important is my Life Lesson: Am I willing to risk feeling uncomfortable and seize the opportunity to break the self-made chains of unworthiness, domination, and fear? In other words, am I willing to hear the answer even when it feels uncomfortable or scary? I believe, as has been proven in the past, that once the phone call is made, my angst will disappear and I will be at peace with my kitchen, my contractor, and most of all, with myself.

Now, I have to add—

5 Make a definite commitment to complete this task (the answer received in #4) by a specific date and time, otherwise we are just fooling ourselves and playing head games.

Clue: To be successful, you cannot skip steps in the formula, any more than you could skip steps in the chemical lab in high school. The one you resist the most is the one that holds your answer.

Someone said, "It works when we work it." Whether you choose to apply it to your Life Problem is your choice, but how do you know if it will work if you don't try it?

ACTION STEPS/YOUR TURN

Who or what are you annoyed with or frustrated at in your life right now, especially that you have been unwilling to address directly? Use the following "Formula For Success" to talk out your problem. You can pretend you are writing to me if that makes it easier. Use extra paper and be ready to make changes in your steps as new insights occur. (I did.) Choose a time when you will be alone and undisturbed for this exercise. Its insights may surprise you, and you can use the formula again and again to solve any puzzling or frustrating Life Problem. You will find an extra copy of this Formula for Success in the back of the book. Feel free to make copies for your future use.

Formula for Success

1 Admit there is a problem. State it briefly here.
   ꙮ

   _____

   _____

   _____

2 Ask for help. (If you are stuck, call a friend you can trust to listen without judgment, and "talk it out.")

3 Accept your part in helping to create it (your Thinker hates this). Write briefly about how you contributed to creating the problem. Be honest, do not leave anything out, or be tempted to shift the blame to another.

∽⊷

_____

_____

_____

4 Be willing to hear the answer, even if it feels uncomfortable or scary.

5 Make a definite commitment to act upon the answer received by a specific day and time, and then sign it, creating a sacred contract with your Higher Power. If you need support to be certain you will follow through and keep your word, call your friend who was willing to listen and support you earlier and ask them to hold you accountable.

Day: **Time:**   **Name:**   **Date:**

PS:I will call the contractor by Monday, June 28, at 6:00 PM.
Nancy B.

I did, and it worked. He came over, answered all my questions honestly, and showed me clearly that it was the color I ordered. It just looked different in high gloss and in a different light. See, all that angst for nothing!

Rule 10

Your Word Has Power.

Our bodies, including our mind and emotions, are life's most magnificent creation. In the Bible, it is written:

"What is man that you are mindful of him. . .you made him a little lower than the heav-

> *"It had long since come to my attention that people of accomplishment rarely sat back and let things happen to them. They went out and happened to things."*
> – Leonardo da Vinci

enly beings and crowned him with glory and honor.

"You made him ruler over the works of your hands, you put everything under his feet."

– Psalms 8: 4-6, New International Version

Nothing on the physical plane surpasses humanity's ability to emulate the Divine, for we duplicate the creative process in co-creating our lives with the Creator itself through the power of the choices we make.

While our bodies appear to be limited by time and space, our minds are not. Our thoughts can travel through other, unseen realms, can imagine things that never have been, and set out to create them. Every time we think, our thoughts fall into the One Mind and are acted upon by the One Creative Power in the entire Universe. That is why it is said that we should be careful what we think because we just might get it. No truer words were ever spoken. Good and bad, positive and negative, building up, or tearing down, all thoughts, not just some and not just the pretty ones or the prayerful ones, reach the Divine ears and the cumulative effect of them tends to manifest in our lives.

All of life lies open to us, ready, willing, and able to fulfill our every desire. If this is true, why is it that we so often suffer, stumble, and fall short of our own highest aspirations to contribute some meaningful good to our world? Perhaps it has to do with asking rightly. If we believe that we are predestined to struggle through life, fighting against unbeatable odds to attain even a modicum of success, then Life fulfills that underlying belief in struggle and allows it to become our reality. If, on the other hand, we believe that Life itself desires to create greater good through us, wants us to succeed, and will guide us to the right people in the right places at the right time to fulfill our desires, then we are consciously working in partnership with the one and only Creative Power in the Universe—and, in time, we are bound to be successful. Suppose we desire to create something that has never been done before, never been wished for, imagined, or pictured. From where does the template for such a design come? Where does the idea itself come from, the inner images and components of an entirely new design if not from our Knower's connection with the One Mind from which all creation springs forth?

Everything in form, everything we can experience with our five senses—sight, sound, touch, taste, and smell—comes from the formless and flows back into it at its demise. Someone once said that "Our bodies are the garages where we park our souls" [author unknown]. Our souls (the formless) give our bodies (the form) life and not the other way around. We, in the Western world, have so aggrandized the physical world through our desires to accumulate "things," including youth, wealth, and power, that we have lost sight of the value of the underlying formless Spirit or Soul that infuses all forms with life and without which all would be dross—dead, lifeless dust.

In Eastern cultures, the formless world of Spirit is accepted and included in daily life just as if it were a sixth sense, as natural and available to all as the other five. If, indeed, all forms, everything that we desire to create in our lives, come from the formless Spirit, how are we to contact it? Where do we begin?

We contact the formless Source of all creation through our own abilities to operate in the field of the formless, through our thoughts, our minds, and our feelings and emotions. A single focused thought backed by the power of emotion, which is energy in motion, reaches the ear of the Infinite, and if held in mind long enough for the needed form to attach itself to the idea, the form will be produced. Some of our inspired ideas seem to manifest in form almost instantly, while others take longer; but if we continue to hold the ideas in place, believing that Life wants us to have them—and that have them we will—they too will come into form in time.

I think of it like ice cube trays. We can fill the trays with any substance we choose, but once we have surrendered them to the freezer, we must wait patiently while the mysterious process takes place in the dark, outside our ability to observe its development. So, too, do we speak our desire or write our affirmations, claiming our greater good, then release them into the mysterious Creative Process that we cannot observe, but can trust, just as we have learned to trust our freezer because we know through experience that it works.

Writing down our goals and reading them aloud daily is a powerful activity in the mind. To begin with, it requires us to become crystal clear regarding what it is we really want. Secondly, in rereading them daily, we may find they need some adjustment; that as we change and grow we may no longer want to move to another state, go back to school, become a doctor, lawyer, or teacher. On the other hand, perhaps our reasons for wanting these things changes and we must be flexible and responsive to those shifts when they occur. Our heart will not lie. When a needed change presents itself, we will benefit by being open to it, but also by testing it through reason, prayer, and time to be certain we are being guided by our heart and not by some ego demand or fear of change.

As we begin to write down our goals, which tend to elicit a genuine commitment on our part, and see them manifesting one after another exactly as we described, we learn to trust the Creative Process and the source from which all good things flow.

When I felt ready to sell our home in Oceanside, California, I wrote the following affirmation, which I read aloud daily:

"I release my home to its new and rightful owners at the perfect right time, at the perfect right price, easily and effortlessly, for the highest good of everyone involved!"

It sold in the first fifteen minutes of the first open house for almost $200,000 more than it would have sold for when I wanted to list it the year before. I invited the couple who purchased it for drinks and hor d'oeuvres and they arrived with a lovely spray of orchids for me. The wife threw her arms around me and thanked me repeatedly for giving them such a magnificent and beautifully maintained home. I had spent a great deal of time and money painting, polishing and shining every nook and cranny, not to get more money, but because I wanted to bless it with my love and appreciation and to pass it on with all the beauty and grace it had provided for my husband and me for twelve wonderful years.

As I prepared myself to look for a new home in a new community, I again wrote down my desires clearly:

"My perfect new home is light-filled and spacious, with a gracious air of welcoming warmth and elegance. It is surrounded by magnificent park-like grounds. I feel totally safe here, am gloriously happy and deeply grateful."

The first thing you may notice if you are not familiar with affirmations is that even though I was weeks away from finding my perfect home, I wrote as if I was already living there. You may also notice that I spoke to the feelings I expected to experience on finding and living in my perfect place, and not to square footage, number of rooms, etc. Life often has a far greater blessing in store for us than we can imagine; therefore, it behooves us to avoid narrowing the field of possibilities by "outlining" exactly what and how our good shall show up. Speak instead to the Big Picture and to the feelings we expect to experience when living our dream or goal.

> *Be impeccable with your word."*
> —Don Miguel Ruiz,
> *The Four Agreements*

My house hunting was disappointing at first. It seemed that everything I could afford was either too tiny, too run-down, or in the wrong place (such as smack up against a freeway!). The first real estate agent I used was disappointing as well—unorganized and poorly prepared—but I was soon led to the perfect agent for me as I continued to speak my affirmation throughout the day, which by then I had memorized.

After signing the escrow papers to release our beautiful home to the perfect couple, and knowing when it would close, I called my new friend and agent and announced that I would buy a home that coming weekend. I intended that our escrow dates would close simultaneously. Therefore, we went out once again and, lo and behold, walked into my perfect new place, and I began to cry. My heart told me that I had come home.

My perfect new home is not only light-filled and spacious (a 1,500-square-foot townhouse), but it looks out on the most expansive park-like grounds imaginable!

No builders in their right minds today would leave so much space between buildings and then fill it with rolling lawns, winding paths, towering trees, and flowers. As I sat in my living room the week after I moved in, surrounded by boxes stacked nearly to the ceiling, and looking out on God's glorious handiwork, I wept in gratitude. Everything I asked for had been fulfilled, and more. I continue to feel this upwelling of joy and gratitude as I step out onto my 20-foot-long balcony up among the trees and thank my Divine Source for my many blessings.

Out of the last ten goals I wrote in the spring, seven have been successfully completed, two were crossed off when I discovered they no longer worked for me, and only one remains to be completed. Writing our goals and reading them daily works!

Action Steps/Your Turn

1 During the next week, decide on ten goals to which you can fully commit.

2 Don't be afraid to include some big ones, but be aware that doing so causes the Universe to move into action to bring them about, so prepare yourself for change.

3 Include some smaller, short-term, but equally satisfying goals.

4 Continue rewriting them until they feel right, until they resonate in your heart.

5 When they are complete, turn to the section marked "Goal Setting" in the back of this book and record your goals there. Fill in the date and sign it.

6 Read your goals morning and night, with feeling, and without fail.

7 As they begin to come into form through your conscious cooperation with the Creative Process, highlight them and write a big "YES!" in the margin, acknowledging that the Universe always says "YES," giving yourself the needed encouragement to continue the process.

8 If you discover, as the weeks go by, that one or more of them no longer fits your new-found direction, cross them off and add others in their place.

9 Be patient, but be persistent. A tomato seed does not grow into a vine and produce ripe tomatoes overnight, but requires attention and care to be productive. Your twice-daily reading of your goals with passion, power, and purpose will water them with your faith into fruition.

Nothing fuels success like success. The completion of even one of your written goals will give you the energy you need to continue to commit daily to accomplishing them all.

Rule 11

If You Can Dream It and Believe It, You Can Achieve It—provided you're willing to do whatever it takes, and never give up until you've reached your goal.

The Universe does not know the difference between big and small. It is as easy for it to create the Alps as it is an anthill. Big and small, hard or easy, are our ideas. The Creative Power

> *"Our creative dreams and yearnings come from a divine source. As we move toward our dreams, we move toward our divinity."*
> — Julia Cameron,
> *The Artists Way*

knows only to do as it is directed by our thoughts. We duplicate the Creative Powers of the Universe itself, only on an individual scale.

In John 1:1, it is written, "In the beginning was the word ...." The initiating act in any new sequence is the thought, the idea, the inspiration, or "the word." Everything begins in the mind. Everything we can see, everything that has ever been created, or ever will be, begins in someone's mind, somewhere. However, in looking back over my life, I realize that I have not always acted on the ideas, the inspirations I have been given.

The tiniest bud on the farthest tip of the highest branch is connected to and fed by the same root system that feeds the massive trunk. The same life force flows through all, big and little, great and small, new beginnings and old stalwarts. Moreover, while the slender veins on the new growth may not seem to carry as great a quantity of that life-giving energy, as it expands and stretches out in new directions, it is able to receive more and thus give more: more shade, more habitat for Nature's creatures, thus contributing to a happier, healthier life on planet Earth.

All our stumbling attempts to try something new—to strike out into new territory—are fed by the same life-force that fuels Microsoft, Donald Trump, and Disneyland. Everyone began at the beginning with just an idea, a hunch, a gut feeling, that "it just might work," and had enough faith in themselves and enough courage to try it. For every mega-success we see in the world, hundreds of thousands more fell by the wayside; but without the courageous souls who took a leap of faith, we would still be walking barefoot and stalking prey in animal skins!

Medical science tells us that one of the best ways we can keep our brains healthy is to learn something new. It matters not a wit if the new thing is bird-watching, a foreign language, or throwing a pot. Even searching for a solution to a sticky problem and not finding it provides healthy, stimulating exercise for our brains.

Our egos want to look good and be perfect in order to elicit ego strokes and our first attempts, whether it is at running a marathon, or painting a portrait, will seldom win a prize. The fear of failure or looking stupid (definitely my ego's greatest fear) has squelched many a brilliant idea in its tracks.

About twenty years ago, as I became newly aware of the need for environmental protection, an idea was given to me as clearly as if I had been handed a blueprint. What I saw were natural canvas bags hanging on a T-stand in the markets. On the bags was the sketch of an endangered tree in green on the left; and on the right was written: "Buy a bag. Save a tree." The idea being that once purchased, we would bring our bags with us each time we

shopped, as they have done in Europe for centuries, thus saving
our forests and reducing waste. However, I knew nothing about
design, manufacturing, or marketing such a product to mammoth
corporations such as Ralph's, Vons, or Albertson's and I didn't
know anyone who did, so I refused to take action. As you can see,
I never forgot it. While I have never seen reusable bags exactly as
I saw them in my mind's eye, some health food markets are sell-
ing them now, and plastic bags were later invented, which at least
shifted our use away from trees to petroleum. I still think the idea
has merit, though it would involve a re-education on our part. We
tend to like things to stay the same and do not want to be incon-
venienced. Who would have guessed that we would be pumping
our own gas and learning to check out our own purchases at
Home Depot? Perhaps someone reading this book will be
inspired by this great idea and bring it to fruition. You have my
blessings. It was just not my cup of tea.

Another idea that did catch fire in me was the One Woman
Show I referred to earlier. After taking voice lessons for a year or
so, and being so encouraged by my teacher to write music and
perform it, I began to ask in my morning meditations what I was
to do with this gift from God. I could not believe it was just for
me to drive an hour each way to sing in my voice teacher's living
room. As I said before, I believe our gifts are to be used to bless
others. I could not do musicals, such as at the Lawrence Welk
Dinner Theater near my home, because my speaking required me
to work on weekends, so I continued to ask, deeply and sincerely.

One morning I heard, "You're going to do a One Woman
Show," and I shouted, "OH NO I'M NOT! I don't know anything
about writing a script, directing, or producing a play. NO! It is
impossible! I can't do it!" However, the idea would not let me go.

It was mine and as terrified as I was at the thought, I was also drawn in with the possibilities, inspired and excited, but I didn't breathe a word to a single soul, not even to Daniel, my wonderful voice coach.

Finally, a week or two later, after I'd gotten a little more used to the idea, I said, once again in my morning meditation: "If this is real, if this is something You (Life) really want me to do, then you are going to have to give me something concrete, something in form so I can see that this is not just a figment of my imagination. Give me something on paper that I can see and hold in my hand so I know it's coming from a Source greater than me."

Immediately it began to pour out onto the page! Scenes, characters, songs—almost as fast as I could write. Every morning, the process continued until I could clearly see the outline of what finally became a two-act, almost two-hour-long original musical production.

I ran across the tape recording of the music lesson in which I told Daniel about my dream. What amazed me was the number of times I said, "I don't know. I don't know how to do it, what a music director is or what they do, how to get accompaniment recorded, and who would do it, and on and on." What I also heard was the joy, the thrill, and my commitment, ignorant and stumbling as it was, to keep fumbling ahead toward my goal. Daniel accepted it all like, well, of course, and answered all my questions patiently and agreed to help in any way he could. He eventually arranged and recorded all the music and became my music director.

As I became more deeply and profoundly committed, the individuals with the necessary talents and abilities began to show up and eagerly climbed on board. The director, who I accidentally sat next to at a summer conference the month before; a fabulous seamstress who'd walked into our church a few weeks earlier, became the wardrobe lady (and later my close friend), creating some fabulous costumes; a choreographer; makeup artist; and on and on—all serendipitously arriving at the precise moment they were needed.

It took nine months (perfect timing for a new birth) to write and stage the production, which was called To Life With Love. In it, I portrayed twelve different characters from Dorothy in the Wizard of Oz, to Marilyn Monroe, to Gloria Estafan. I even wrote the theme song, I Have a Dream, which, of course, I had also never done before. We put on three performances, all nearly sold out, and I soared past all my fears to pour out all the love and joy in me through song, dance, and acting. I pulled out all the stops and went for broke.

> *"Each one of us matters, has a role to play and makes a difference."*
> — Dr. Jane Goodall, *Reason for Hope*

That was four years ago and people are still talking about how astounded they were at so professional a production when most expected it to be only a nice little recital. One of our guests, who manages recording artists, was overheard to say, "It was a touch of Broadway."

My point in sharing the details about the excellence of the production and the performance is certainly not to toot my own horn. It is, instead, to clearly point out that it was not I, myself, not my Thinker, my everyday logical, reasoning mind that created it. It was, instead, the connection of my Knower to the one Infinite Mind who knows all things and indwells all things, and who answers our sincere prayers when we turn to it and humbly ask for guidance and direction, and then be willing to follow the guidance we receive.

I do not have any desire whatsoever to be a business tycoon, a manufacturer of shopping bags and such; but there is in me a performer, a soul that sings with joy at the prospect of pouring out the great love in me through song, dance, or acting, to lift up and bless others. I have been doing it since I was a toddler and nothing warms my heart and fills me with joy like feeling the Spirit move in and through me to connect with an audience in such depth that they can literally feel the Spirit of joy moving in them as well.

Know that this same Creative Power is available to you to fulfill your greatest dreams, your highest aspirations, your wildest imaginings, if you are willing to commit your whole heart and soul, to ask deeply every morning in quiet meditation for your right path, the path that only you can take, the creative endeavor that only you can bring forth.

No one else could have written and performed To Life With Love exactly the way I did, and no one else can live your life for you, create your dream for you, or give you your goal. You alone can plumb the deep recesses of your soul and uncover the hidden treasures buried there. You can do it—with the help of your Knower and the guidance and creative genius of the one all-knowing Mind.

ACTION STEPS/YOUR TURN

1 Set aside some specific time every morning or evening to sit in quiet meditation and contemplation and begin to ask what is next for you to do, how you can serve the world in a greater way, what gifts your soul came here to give.

Yes, I know it is hard with kids and lunches to prepare and school and work, but if you are truly committed to stepping out in faith, you will find a way. I used to sit on the floor in our tiny half-bath with the door locked. It was the only place I knew I could have some privacy in our busy household filled with the happy sounds of children and the morning's activities.

2 Keep a pad and pen at your side to jot down briefly any new ideas or suggestions that catch your attention; then go back to the silence.

3 Relax. Do not try to make it happen. Listening in the silence may not be something you've been trained to do, so be patient with yourself. Just sit; ask; and listen.

4 Don't give up if you do not hear something profound in the first week or so. It takes time to develop relationships, and if this is a new experience for you, you will need time to learn to still the Thinker who wants to fill your pad of paper quickly with a "to do" list and get back to the busyness of the day.

Resist it.

5 Once again, following through on the guidance you receive about the little things will build your confidence and the trust you will need when the bigger things begin to surface.

6 Try especially hard to do those things you instantly resist. This is different from choosing not to manufacture bags. When we find ourselves digging our emotional heels in, it is usually the ego again trying to control us and stop us from changing or moving in a new direction, which it sees as a threat to its existence and its ability to continue to control our lives and to keep us small!

7 When you finally feel that you have hit the big one, do not share it with a single soul, at least not at first. The bigger it is the more concentrated energy you will need to stay focused in order to bring it into form.

8 When you do decide to share it, make certain that the person you confide in sees even bigger possibilities for you than you can see for yourself. Again, ask for guidance as to who this person might be if you are not sure.

9 Don't talk about it. Keep it to yourself. Keep it between you and your Creator who will give you each step when you are ready for it and not before. If I had seen every step I would need to bring my dream into reality all at once, I would never have had the courage to begin, to take that first baby step.

10 If your dream seems overwhelming, break it down into bite-sized pieces and write them down as you become aware of them, following the goal-setting formula in Rule #10.

11 Know that you will face challenges, be frustrated, and possibly overwhelmed or exhausted at times, and want to quit. Just keep your vision clearly in mind and keep moving ahead one-step at a time.

Know that if it is yours to do, everything you need will be provided at the right time and in the right place by the right person or persons.

Example:

I was an advisor for the first time at our church's National Teen Summer Camp and there was a lot to learn. Three other advisors and I led the pre-teen family groups with two daily meetings, including lessons, crafts, and activities. All of the others had years of experience and knew what they were doing almost without speaking, and I was often left feeling in the dark and totally unclear and unprepared regarding what I was to do with my group of ten boys and girls.

I spoke with the director about my concerns, particularly regarding being left alone at one time with two groups (twenty kids) with no instructions and no crafts prepared. I thought we clearly understood each other, so when the same thing happened the third time, I lost it! I did not want to do it anymore, was angry, frustrated, and on the verge of tears.

I went to a minister friend for prayer and comfort and felt much better when I left, only to walk directly into the person I most did not want to see right then. Nevertheless, I realized that my Knower (or the Great Knower) had put her right where she need-ed to be. Therefore, I took a deep breath, said a quick, silent prayer, walked up to her and said, "We need to talk."

As we stepped outside, the other two advisors miraculously appeared and within just a few minutes, amends were made, the air was cleared, and we recommitted to working together for the good of the children, and to support each other with love. From that moment on, everything worked smoothly and efficiently, with excellent communication and cooperation all around. If I had given in to my resistance, I would have missed the opportu-nity to initiate a healing that was deeply needed by all of us, including the director, who was feeling unappreciated.

The emotional upsets we leave unresolved come back to haunt us in another face and another situation until we face them and heal them, so the sooner the better. Do it now!

Rule 12

When life gets you down and you are stuck in the pits... Get Up, Get Out, and Get Going!

With the death of my husband, my rich, full, secure life was suddenly flipped upside down. Even after coming to grips with "being alone with just me," I still find myself deeply lonely and wallowing in a pity party from time to time.

> "Merely accepting this simple truth about ourselves—that we are stuck—is the elegant choice, the best way to get unstuck. The part-that-knows knows if we need outside help after our initial self-acceptance."
> — Jennifer James, Ph.D., *Twenty Steps to Wisdom*

My broken heart wants to sleep late, starve, or overeat, get lost in sappy novels or soap operas, and support the facial tissue industry by weeping buckets over absolutely nothing at all. The "poor me" still surfaces now and then, although it is certainly not as frequent. Recently, I found myself playing out such a "soap opera" scenario in my new home. My new DSL was slower than molasses after four visits from SBC technicians; the phone would not pick up messages but went straight to the fax, which they swore it would not do; my 42-inch TV died and the new Dish had to be moved, since it had been installed incorrectly. Nothing earth-shaking, to be sure, yet every time I called for assistance from the separate SBC installers of all three, I felt unreasonably emotional, got nowhere, and my malaise deepened. Therefore, I sat myself down and asked, "What is going on?"

I finally got it. My husband was a self-made techie. He loved sitting for hours, weeks, months with a prickly installation or programming problem. He would wait on hold for an hour-and-a-half to discuss with a real techie the terms written in the very small print in the back of a manual. It got his neurons crackling and firing all over the place. It was exciting and ever-so gratifying when he finally figured it out and arrived at a solution all by himself.

> *"To journey, you must first go out."*
> – The Oculatum

My take on the whole electronics thing was: You figure out how to make it work and when you've got all the bugs out, show me the button to push. I must have other talents because patience for this kind of stuff was left out of my package. So what is going on, as I reach for a second box of tissues, is—

I MISS MY HUSBAND!

The guy who could fix anything with a hammer, a screwdriver, and a staple gun; the guy with the patience of Job, the deep voice of James Earl Jones, the looks of Robert Preston (for whom he was often mistaken), and the warm body I could plant my frozen feet on with hardly ever a complaint.

It's hard to see what's really going on while we're the main character stuck in our own melodramatic plot. We have to become an observer, to get outside of the story so we can look at it with mild interest, but without emotional attachment. The solution is:

Get up, Get Out, and Get Going!

Find someone, anyone, who is in worse—real—circumstances than your soap opera character and give them a hand. I took my four- and six-year-old granddaughters to McDonald's for lunch and the playground to give their pregnant mother a break and then stayed to help put out a mailing for their in-home business. I went for walks, hired a locksmith and TV repairman to handle some of the "honey-dos," and began to feel like life was doable, even enjoyable, again.

When your emotions seem to be working overtime, whatever is bubbling up on the surface is never the problem. The real culprit lies buried deep in your subconscious and waits to be coaxed to the surface with gentle questioning and patient listening. The alternative is to continue slamming doors, muttering obscene phrases under your breath—all the while working up a good case of acid indigestion!

Action Steps/Your Turn

1   **Get Up!** The more we give in to our doldrums, the deeper we dig our pit and the harder it is to climb out. Somebody needs you today! No matter how bad it is, we would not trade it for another's misery, so Get Up! Praise your legs that walk, your arms that reach, and your eyes that see. Call a friend, someone you know who needs a lift, and give generously of your time and caring. You may even forget why you were feeling so blue.

2   **Get Out!** Nothing shifts our energy like getting out in Nature. If all else fails, go shopping! When my dear cousin awoke on the one-year anniversary of her husband's death, she said to herself, "Sally (name changed), you can lie in bed and cry all day, or you can get up, get dressed, and go somewhere." As much as she hates the mall, she dressed in her best outfit and spent the entire day there! It was far better than the alternative and it got her through one of the most difficult days in her life.

3   **Get Going!** Get excited about a project of your own. Clean out a flowerbed and plant something new. Change your hair color and get a new lease on life. Repaint your bedroom. Dye your curtains or make some new ones. You need a change, so create one!

Rule **13**

Become as a little child and . . . Let Yourself Play!

By that, I do not mean that we are to drool, wet our pants, or throw tantrums. I mean, instead, that we are to allow ourselves to be captivated with the wonders of Life all

"There are two ways to live your life. One is as though nothing is a miracle; the other is as though everything is a miracle."
— Albert Einstein

around us. To lie on our stomachs in the grass, watching an inchworm measure a lily pad, and marvel at the way its body works and wonder if we could do that too. To gaze in awe at the everchanging pattern and colors of a sunset ablaze at the beach as the sun turns the ocean into a glittering, undulating carpet of diamonds and then watch, holding our breath, as the giant orange ball slips silently out of sight; to count the stars and make a wish on one. In other words, to find our way back to the awe and appreciation for Life itself—in all its wondrous and myriad forms.

Children play hard at whatever they are doing. They run, build, tear down, climb, wrestle, sing, and dance, throwing everything they've got into the moment's experience, then drop it when it no longer holds their interest and go exploring for their next adventure. Their imaginations are without bounds and they question everything: "What is it?" "How does it work?" "Why?" "Why not?" "How come?"

The one thing I've noticed recently with my youngest grand-children (I'll have twelve and three greats by Christmas) is how they love to build something up, as big and high and colorful as possible, and then tear it down with glee to make something new and different or better!

Businesses began exploring this approach with their TQM (Total Quality Management) process in the '80s and '90s, which asked not how can we make a better widget, or even how can we make another half cent per widget, but why do we make widgets at all?

What if we began asking ourselves that most basic question regarding our businesses, our homes, and our relationships, to help us remember the underlying desires we sought to fulfill when we first dreamed our dreams so long ago. Perhaps we sought to share our talents, to give our gifts in the case of busi-ness, and now instead of the joy of giving, we find ourselves over-whelmed with paperwork, permits, and the ponderosity of man-agement and finance.

Our dream for our primary love relationship was to give and receive love, to fill and be fulfilled by the amazing gift of sexual union in which all the cares of the day seem to melt away—not to wrangle over who forgot to take the trash out or pay the light bill. Our homes were to be our sanctuaries where we came together to reconnect, regroup, and refresh ourselves, a sacred space that nurtured our souls. Sometimes they seem to have become more like demanding two-year-olds, that no matter how much time, energy, and attention we give them, it's never enough—and the "honey-do" list just grows longer and longer.

If we do not take the time to nurture the relationships, which are the nexus of our homes, no amount of extreme makeovers will be able to bridge the chasms of separation and misunderstanding that can ferment as we grow silently apart.

Action Steps/Your Turn

1 Reintroduce the idea of play into your life. Play does not conjure up images of competitive sports, although they can certainly work for you. To me, play feels more free form, not so structured. Ask your kids or friends' kids for suggestions. You might invite some over and:

    a Sleep in the backyard under the stars.

    b Tell stories in your PJs on the floor by the fireplace or around a fire pit.

    c Roast marshmallows and make Someores with graham crackers and a chocolate bar.

    d Make French toast on an upside-down juice can (paper removed, please!) over a sterno can or candle in the backyard.

    e Play in the rain, make mud pies with some kids, and get wet, get dirty. Do sidewalk chalk art or finger-painting.

Our grandkids wrote "Welcome home, Grandpa!" on our driveway with chalk when he came home after heart surgery, and we never washed it off. It stayed for about six months and warmed his heart every time he saw it.

2 If you are in a committed relationship, plan regular date nights, especially if you have children in your home. If you cannot afford a sitter, trade off with friends. No matter how noisy or demanding the extra kids can be for an afternoon or evening, the rewards will be great when you and your loved one have time alone to rekindle your romance.

3 If you are in a long-term committed relationship, suggest setting aside some time to:

a Come together to discuss your long-term goals as partners. Share your hopes and dreams, any disappointments
and desires for change.

b Take a week to search deeply in your hearts and jot
down some ideas, some suggestions to reawaken the pas-
sions, the dreams that brought you together in the first
place.

c Come together again and share your ideas. Discuss
them—compromise, make adjustments, and try to come up
with at least one or two you can both commit to with
enthusiasm and without hesitation.

d Write them out as simply as possible, in one sentence
each, then sign and date them and put them somewhere
you will see them daily, perhaps on your bathroom mirror.

4 Look at your established habits or customs and ask yourself if
they are as fulfilling today as when they first began. If you can
honestly say that they are not, don't be afraid to tear them
down with glee to create something even better in their
place—even if you have no idea at the moment what that
"better" might be.

5 Start a collection of cartoons and jokes and put them in a little spiral-bound notebook so you can flip it open to a new,
funny, or inspiring one.

6 *SURPRISE YOUR BELOVED* and yourself. Create a surprise
overnight stay at a local hotel or motel, again trading with
another family for childcare if necessary. Planning your secret

getaway will keep you energized for weeks, and whatever happens before the big day—don't tell. It will make you feel like a kid again.

7 Congratulations! You are doing great! Now that you got the idea, jot down some creative ideas of your own.

I can hear your frustrated questions now: "How am I supposed to find time to play when I don't have enough time to do everything I need to do already?"

I can't honestly answer that question for each of you because I don't know your personal situations, but I can tell you this—that ten or twenty minutes of pure play—dancing in the living room in your underwear to a hot Latin beat (with the shades down, please!)—can make the rest of your day flow like the music. We accomplish more in less time when we are fresh, energized, and fully engaged in the task at hand. When we free ourselves to dance, laugh, make love or mud pies with joyous abandon in the moment, our next moments, whether they be paying the bills, scrubbing the floor, or making a sale will also feel more alive, more joyous. *Note:If it makes you feel really silly and somewhat giggly inside or embarrassed, you are right on target, so—*

GO FOR IT!

All you've got to lose is that stodgy, workaholic, perfectionist, stick-in-the-mud character you're so familiar with, so start tearing down that society-created image and recreate yourself in your own image. Your business and your relationships will blossom in the glow of your newfound *joie de vivre*.

LOVE LIFE AND LIFE WILL LOVE YOU BACK!

Rule 14

We don't see what is...
We See What We
Expect To See.

Our eyes can play tricks on us because they are operated upon by our mind—either the Thinker or the Knower—and often what we see is determined not by what is there, but by what we *expect* to be there.

The hills around my former home in Oceanside,

"The brain does not know the difference between what it sees and what it remembers. It calls up the neural net of past experiences and uses them as a model of the present."
— Dr. Joseph Dispenza,
What the Bleep

California, were under constant development and those responsible were forever creating new roads through the hills where there were none before. One particular future road intersected at a stoplight on my regular route and from time-to-time, over a twelve-year period, the earthmovers would begin their ant-like circling, once again picking up and laying down dirt, as the space between the two hills grew ever more road-like. Since it had continued for so many years, I had come to expect this activity as an interesting diversion on an otherwise ordinary section of a frequently traveled road.

One day, while sitting at the stoplight, I was stunned to see cars passing in front of me and proceeding up the hill, which was now a fully completed divided highway with palm trees marching up and over the hill into the distance! How was this possible? How could I have missed the weeks and months of changed activity required to alter the landscape and allow such a tremendous change to take place? I cannot tell you how baffled I was, how confused I felt, how utterly dumbfounded to think I could have missed the whole thing. Since I had come to *expect* the same type of activity there over time, did I just not look, or did I look and *not see?*

More importantly, is it possible that we may be sleepwalking through life, missing opportunities being offered to us for advancement, greater happiness, fulfillment, or success because we *expect things to stay the same.* Are we not awake enough to perceive the shift when it comes and the opening it provides for greater participation in Life through the sharing of our unique gifts in a greater way?

Have you ever had the experience of coming home after a long vacation and feeling like someone painted all the houses, widened the street, and planted new flowers while you were away? I have, and that is the difference between being awake and asleep. Life has more color, more aliveness, and is more exciting and inviting when we are awake. Charles Filmore, the co-founder of the Unity Spiritual movement, wrote late in his nineties:

"I am alive, awake, aware, joyous and enthusiastic about life!"

I cannot think of a better affirmation to begin every day.

If we desire to expand our sphere of influence, we must expose ourselves to new, even challenging, experiences on a regular basis. Edwene Gaines rose from poverty to become a well- known, in demand, highly successful biblical teacher of prosperity and abundance. A delightful, entertaining "Southern belle" and senior citizen, she sets herself a challenge each year—A BIG RISK—to make certain she is alive, awake, aware, and fully engaged in life in the greatest way possible. In short, she does not intend to miss a single thing: from rappelling 200 feet down into a black cave, to flying high off the roof of the Stratosphere Hotel in Las Vegas, to traveling alone through the jungles of Peru to meet with a real shaman—if she hasn't done it all yet, by the time she leaves this planet you can bet your bottom dollar she will!

The danger in sleepwalking through life, expecting things to remain the same, is that we miss being truly awake in each moment and experiencing it fully. Have you ever lost something like your keys or a piece of jewelry and looked in the same drawer two or three times, only to go back again in desperation to discover it was there all along, right before your eyes? We wonder how it got there, or who put it there when we were not looking. The truth is it was there all the time—it had to be—but our Thinker cannot accept that, so it makes up something with which it is more comfortable. Is it possible that we could not see what we were looking for because we did not *expect* to find it there? Why is it that when we have made a mistake running a long column of numbers that we tend to make the same mistake repeatedly? Is it because we are "seeing" it the way we expect it to be? It sometimes takes someone else, with a new eye, to see it correctly.

We think thousands of thoughts every day; the discouraging thing is that most of them are the same ones we thought yesterday. We can become so accustomed to this repetitive, hypnotic way of thinking that when a new, exciting, challenging idea breaks through, our first reaction may be to discount it, fluff it off, or ignore it. All of us have been given "ideas," inventions, if you will, to create something new that has never been done before. Most of these ideas, which I believe are messages from our Knower, have gone by the wayside, but we do not forget them.

To understand that life is a flow, not fixed or static, encourages us to live fully in the moment, to accept, appreciate, and then release the beautiful, fun, exciting, or awful experiences that find their way into our lives with gratitude and joy. All of our belongings, the things we treasure, are not ours to keep—we simply use them and pass them on. Sooner or later, all our "toys," our family heirlooms, books, trinkets, and treasures will reside somewhere else—our ring on someone else's hand, our family pictures gracing another wall, as other faces we may not now know relate our history, the events that made up our lives, to those yet unborn.

ACTION STEPS/YOUR TURN

1 TRY SOMETHING NEW! To enliven your senses and wake up your spirit of adventure: try new food, new friends, new exercise or entertainment, a new route to work, or how you spend your weekends.

2 VOLUNTEER with a youth group, at the hospital, library, or senior citizen center.

3 GET UP EARLIER, watch a sunrise or sunset, get carried away by the ever-changing colors, the majesty, the immensity of the Universe we live in and the intricately woven sense of order flowing through all of Nature from the birthing of babies to the changing seasons, to the ripening of fruit on the trees, to the beating of our hearts—all given to us freely and continuously from that great heart of Love and the overflow of abundance from our Creator.

> *"Let your whole life be a walking hymn of praise and gratitude and you will experience a shift so profound the depth and joy of which you never could have dreamed."*
> — anonymous

4 BE GRATEFUL. Take nothing for grant, from your eyes that allow you to perceive beauty, to your ears that hear music and laughter, to your own voice (be sure to use it to voice appreciation and to uplift), to the water you drink and the bed in which you sleep.

5 GIVE THINGS AWAY! If you have not used it, worn it, or seen it for one to two years, you do not need it anymore. It is taking up space in your energy field that could be put to better use. Letting go of "stuff," especially the expensive stuff, the things we spent "too much on" or have an attachment to, creates space for something new to come in. We breathe easier, feel lighter, and are blessed because we have blessed another by passing our "stuff" along to them.

Rule 15

Be a Joy Bringer.

My dear friend, Bill Hansen, author of *Hope Heals*, has beaten Parkinson's disease and prostate cancer with a protocol that includes mind, spirit, and body. I am privileged to have watched this amazing man's vision of getting his message of *hope* to the world

> *"Ignore appearances as best you can and lie back singing in the everlasting arms. The healing will come spontaneously as your consciousness floats upward to touch the edge of mine."*
> — Ruby Nelson,
> *The Door of Everything*

become a reality through the publishing of his book and all the challenges that were faced and overcome because his passion for the vision was so much bigger than he was.

From being unable to roll over in bed, having to regurgitate food because his throat muscles could no longer swallow, and thus losing twenty-five pounds, *he made a decision* to fight it with everything he had and *never to quit*, no matter what! Today, even though he monitors his energy closely and carefully controls *everything* that goes into his mind and body, Bill Hansen is one of the most energetic, passionately alive people I know. He works with a trainer three times a week and dances twice a week, while running his company, MJB Global, and promoting his book.

Every time we meet, he brings me some inspiring quotes, affirmations on health, prosperity, or creating your own vision. This is the step in his *Hope Heals* protocol that blew me away. *"I wake up with this intention every day: to bring joy to others."*

"We are rich only through what we give, and poor only through what we refuse."
– Anne Swetchine

By focusing his *attention* through his *intention* to bring joy into *other* people's lives, he was able to shift his energy away from his own fears of a horrifying death, to seek to fulfill the needs of others.

Because we are designed to give love and therefore joy to others, we cannot be truly happy or content inside unless we are doing so. In addition, it would be extremely difficult, if not impossible, to give joy to others while we are worried or fear-filled inside. Joy bubbles up inside from a heart filled with gratitude and that takes conscious effort, a decision on our part. Yes, there are those days when circumstances cause our hearts to sing, but what about the difficult days when our bodies ache or our heart is broken, or we are fired or receive "bad news"? Unless we set a conscious intention at the beginning of every day, and we revisit that intention throughout the day, the ordinary wear and tear of life can pull us down.

A traffic jam on the freeway that causes us to miss an important meeting can ruin our day before it begins unless we have set a *conscious* intention to find the good in *every* situation. Perhaps in this case it could be that it was not your car that crashed and turned over on the freeway. Perhaps it could be that it is not you or your loved ones speeding away in the ambulance to some unknown future in the hospital. Instead of giving in to fear and frustration, we can choose to take those unexpected quiet moments to bless those around us, to have empathy for those involved in any accident or mishap, to even look up and appreciate the beauty of the day and breathe in deeply the sweet breath of life.

It is easy to write these words as I sit in my favorite "writing" chair in my beautiful new bedroom in the cool of the morning, but it is not always easy to carry it out in the heat of the day.

Action Steps/Your Turn

1 On a scale of one to ten, ten being the greatest, where would you say your Joy factor is today?

1_____10

2 If you need more Joy in your life, consider "priming the Joy pump" by giving some away today.

3 Who do you know that needs some Joy today? Someone at work, or in your family? Call them up, right now, and generate some genuine Joy for them, especially if you do not feel like it. Give some encouragement or praise for a job well done, or even for a sincere effort. They will try ten times as hard next time if they think their efforts were appreciated.

4 After speaking with your selected "Joy receiver," measure your own "Joy factor" again, on the same scale of one to ten. Notice if it has moved, and acknowledge yourself for making a difference in someone's life.

1_____10

5 Consider setting an intention each day to be a Joy giver.

See how many people you can give Joy to in a single day! You will be amazed at the number of opportunities that are available to give Joy once you start looking for them.

Rule 16

Clean up, confess, ask forgiveness for, and let go of all guilty secrets.

Guilty secrets, festering in the dark, eat away at our joy of life; create havoc in our body system, and block our creativity, which is our connection to our great Knower!

I carried a guilty secret in my heart for two and a half years. I shudder now as I tap into those dark feelings once

"When something looks like it isn't right, then it's a pit stop on the way to rightness. Our lives are headed toward one fulfillment after another. ... Any turbulence along the journey will be later seen to have been meaningful and good."
— Rev. Dr. Jesse Jennings

again. For some reason, perhaps because I needed to share this painful lesson with you, it was thrust foremost into my consciousness this week. It was time to face it and clean it up, because it would not let me go.

The day before my husband died, I had called all the kids and told them the seriousness of his illness, and they all came to visit, except the youngest son, who felt that his family, with two young children, would be too much for "Dad," so out of concern for his father, he elected to come the following day. Later that night, after everyone left, he called to speak with his father. However, Dick was miserable and angry as the male nurse tried to make him more comfortable. I remember sitting with the phone in my hand and *deliberately* letting my beloved son wait, and wait, and wait in silence (out of my own anger and frustration), not communicating what was going on, until he finally said, "The movie is starting now, so I guess I'll call back tomorrow." However, tomorrow never came.

When I got the call at 5:00 AM the next morning to come to the hospital, I discovered that Dick had pulled the oxygen off during the night and by the time they found him, he had suffered extensive brain damage. When our young son arrived, he was beside himself for not having seen or spoken with his dad the day before. As I watched him suffer, I realized the enormity and consequences of what I had done, but I hid behind my grief and did not immediately assuage his guilt by telling him the truth. I remember him saying, "Someday I'll tell you [why he was suffering so]."

As time went by, he continued to miss his dad so much that he would call repeatedly to hear his father's voice on our answering machine. Each time he mentioned it, my conscience hurt, and I was reminded that he still carried an unnecessary burden of guilt on his heart that I had the power to release with just a few words. However, the longer I put it off, the deeper the shame became. To think that I could allow my son to continue to suffer was so unconscionable as to silence my tongue.

This week, when I could tolerate the pain and shame no longer, I called and asked to meet with him alone. I said I had a confession to make and I needed to ask his forgiveness. When my confession spilled out, I was stunned to hear him say, "But I *did* speak to him that night. The reason I was so upset was that his last words to me were angry, very angry." He went on to say he'd been sitting in a movie theater with his wife waiting for the movie to begin when he called and that when it started, he felt it would be rude to continue speaking and so hung up, and that's when his Dad blew up. *I don't remember any of this!!* It is as if we were two people having two completely different experiences of the same thing. I could not believe it! All those years of unnecessary suffering. What a colossal, sinful waste of precious life-energy that could have been put to better use. Now I could choose to punish myself for another two years by being guilty for feeling guilty, or I can choose to *let it all go!*

Now that some time has passed and I have let it go, I can honestly say that I am grateful. Grateful that our son did speak to his father before he died; grateful that I did not deliberately cause him pain; and grateful for this lesson that I will never forget!

The Bible says, "… let not the sun go down upon your wrath." (Ephesians 4:26) The wrath, the rage and shame that you feel against yourself because of your oh-so-human faults, is just as unforgivable as your wrath against another. You are a precious offspring of the Creator, and you deserve to be happy, harmonious, and free. Do not give in to self-flagellation. It gains you no brownie points in Heaven. Gaining "heavenly points" comes from having a clean heart, being right with your Creator and all of Its Creation–including yourself. Be kind to yourself, as kind as you would be to a misbehaving child who is trying to learn how to live in the world. We are all still learning and growing. Life is a process, not a destination, and when we have learned all we came here to learn, we will leave this earthly planet and go on to other adventures, other learning in another place and time.

> *"In the process, while we are learning, we are still perfect as we are."*
> — Carol Winicur, R.Sc.P.

Action Steps/Your Turn

1 If you feel you have done something wrong, made a mistake, been thoughtless, or deliberately hurtful, clean it up! Go to the person and get it all out. Do not hold anything back.

2 Do it quickly—the sooner the better. The longer you put it off, the more energy it gains until it feels impossible and unforgivable. It is not.

3 Practice cleaning up the little stuff immediately! When you make a habit of confessing your small mistakes instantly, handling the big stuff when it comes along will become easier.

4 Forgive yourself. If you find that your transgression, which in your mind was so huge, was no big thing, or even totally forgotten by its recipient, let it go. Do not use it as another opportunity to punish yourself ad nauseam.

5 Honor yourself. Begin to honor the channel for creativity that you are on earth. Make a decision to keep your channel open and clear of any old, outworn stories of guilt or shame.

6 Set yourself free. Notice how much lighter you feel after releasing those burdens from your heart. Be aware that carrying such burdens weighs heavily on the beautifully designed organ of your heart, and decide to make its job easier by eliminating all unnecessary burdens.

Rule

Don't Dream Away Time: Be Productive.

For a long time after my husband died, I felt lost, directionless, and I prayed often for guidance. Where would I go? What was I to do? What was the rest of my life on earth supposed to be about? Moreover, even, in

> *"It doesn't interest me what you do for a living. I want to know what you ache for and if you dare to dream of meeting your heart's longing."*
> — Oriah Mountain Dreamer, *The Invitation*

the context of my new, unexpected "widowhood," *who was I*, not as part of a couple, but as a single woman on my own for the very first time in my life? From time to time, I tried to step out in a new direction, but it always fell through and I was back where I started. Don't get me wrong—I was doing what I was doing before and doing it well, with commitment, discipline, and sincerity, sometimes even joyously, but underneath it felt like I was slogging through mud, going through the motions.

Then it happened. I went to one of our favorite eateries, The Happy Noodle, that I hadn't been to since Dick died, and the answer I'd been looking for came in a fortune cookie: *Do not allow yourself to dream away time—be productive.*

It could not have been clearer if it had been written in neon lights on the side of the Empire State Building, and I knew it was meant just for me. The message to me was:

TAKE ACTION!
STOP WASTING TIME!
DO IT NOW!

WOW! I jumped into gear and immediately began cleaning out closets, cupboards, and drawers, preparing to make a move—where to I did not know and it did not matter. I had something to do and I was doing it. I had broken out of the lethargy, and I was not going to give in to it again. I called our kids and told them the dining room was packed full of family treasures for them to divide amongst themselves and take home. I polished all of the silver and washed the crystal stemware I had not used in years and took armloads of clothing to the local thrift shop. It felt so good to let go and lighten up. Mostly, though, it felt good to be doing something instead of being stuck in the muddle of trying to figure out what to do.

I contacted a real estate agent and found and made an appointment with a personal coach to talk about the book idea that had been languishing on a backburner since it was given to me by my Knower shortly after Dick's death (the one I thought I was writing when this one came through). I was on the move, taking action, and it felt GREAT!

Action Steps/Your Turn

1 Be productive! Drag out that wonderful creative idea, the one that scared you or made your heart sing, and take some action on it.

2 Do some research on the Internet. There is a whole world of information out there just waiting for you. Use it!

3 Take a risk. Call someone you would never think to call who might help. Even if they say no, the energy of your willingness to risk and your commitment to taking action will fuel your next step.

4 Make an appointment with a mentor/coach/counselor that will guide you, encourage you, keep you focused, and help you keep your word.

5 Do it NOW! Today! Feel the creative energy begin to flow again. Feel fully alive again. Get excited, *but keep it to yourself!*

The surest way to deflate your creative balloon is to share it with someone who is not on your wavelength. You will need every ounce of creative juices you possess to bring your Spirit-inspired, God-idea into form. So do not waste a single drop. Nurture this little seedling idea; handle it gently and with loving care. Do not expose it to the harsh elements of the criticism and doubt of others. If you *do* decide to share it, be certain that it is only with someone who sees an even bigger picture for you than you can see for yourself.

Rule 18

Just Do It — Don't Judge It.

Judging your work is not your job. Your job is to do the work you have been given in the best possible way you can, and to let others decide its worth.

As a new speaker and teacher of spiritual truths some years ago, it suddenly struck me one day that there was only one thing to say:

> *"What we have to contribute is unique and irreplaceable. What we withheld from life is lost to life. The entire world depends on individual choices."*
> — Duane Elgin

There is only ONE LIFE.
It flows through everything, including you and me.
It pours out Its good gifts without limit and without end.

THAT'S IT! The whole ball of wax! How was it possible for me to create such a unique, inspiring, and convincing way to communicate these universal truths that lives would be transformed, broken relationships mended, and broken bodies healed—for this was my sacred commitment and anything less would be and is unacceptable? While I *knew* that such transformational healings were possible—because I had experienced them many times myself—who was I to believe that such healing power could flow through me for the benefit of others?

Marianne Williamson wrote,

> *"We were born to make manifest the glory of God*
> *that is within us.*
> *It is not just in some of us, it is in everyone."*

Made in the image and after the likeness of our Creator, is it not possible that *all* of us have this power, this ability to inspire, lift up, heal, and bless? Perhaps we cannot yet walk on water or raise someone from the dead, but our smile can warm a lonely soul's heart, our listening can ease a troubled friend, and our prayers can comfort a friend in need. A kiss on a skinned knee helps make the pain go away; and a strong, steady hand and willing heart can help another navigate through troubled waters.

> *"No one ever built a monument to a critic."*
> – George Bernard Shaw

We look too far and wide for complicated solutions to difficult problems when the simple gifts we all have to give—our smile, a hug, a listening ear, our friendship, our willingness to stand by during troubled times—are the gifts of healing with which we all have been blessed. To judge them as less than good, or less than worthy is to judge the work of our Creator who blessed us with them as less than good.

It is also true that our smiles, our friendship, are not always met with appreciation or even acceptance. Sometimes we find our gifts refused, walked upon, or rebuffed. Again, it is not our job to judge another's response. We do not know what is in their mind, what they are going through. Our job is to give as our hearts guide us to do, then let it go. Perhaps our willingness to shine our light *does* make a difference that we cannot see. Perhaps it gives someone food for thought and causes him or her to shift their perspective just a little.

You do not have to be a millionaire, a movie star, or a brain surgeon to make a difference in the world. Some people who have made the greatest difference in the world were simple people who chose to do simple tasks, well.

Mother Theresa said, "There are no great acts, only small acts done with great love."

A corporate executive who moved to a small Midwest town when he retired, was bored and listless, so he searched for something to do. However, in this small town there was no work for a retired executive. There was just one job available, it was for a custodian at the local high school. After some time passed, and finding nothing else opening up, he decided to take it.

The town had its share of toughs and gangs, and as he discovered, many came from broken homes where there was no father in the home. Over time, he began to like these young boys, who were trying so hard to be tough, and he made himself available to them. They began opening up to him, to trust and confide in him. They affectionately named him Gramps, and I feel certain that more lives were changed by Gramps as the friendly custodian than were ever changed by the corporate executive in a highly paid position. The payoff was certainly not his paycheck, but the love and respect he received from these young men and the warmth in his heart, knowing that his simple gifts steered many young lives away from an aimless and perhaps violent life to one of purpose. [author unknown]

ACTION STEPS/YOUR TURN

1 What are your natural gifts? The things about you that people comment on most often that you tend to disallow as unimportant. Do you give service far beyond what is required and call it ordinary? Do you have the gift of making others feel special? Is it your smile, your light-hearted way of making messy situations a little easier to get through? You know what they are. List them here. It is not being conceited. It is honoring the gifts your soul came here to give.

ເ◆

_____

_____

_____

_____

_____

_____

2 Sit in the silence for a few moments and breathe deeply and slowly, then ask yourself this question and let the answer come from your heart.

If you could give one gift to the world before you leave the planet, what would it be?

Notice that it probably had very little to do with your bank account, or your accumulation of "things." The gifts we came here to give come from our hearts; so status, wealth, position have no bearing on our ability to give them. All that is required is our willingness to listen to the inner voice we can hear only when we get quiet, and to follow its simple guidance. In doing so, we bless not only the planet but also ourselves, for we are acting in alignment with our soul's purpose and therefore harmony reigns throughout our body temple, mind, and affairs.

3 On a separate piece of paper, write a letter from Life, acknowledging you for the above-mentioned gifts you have contributed to the world as if they were already done. Begin it with:

Dear (your name):
In recognition of the following gifts of the Spirit you have con-
tributed to the world,
(And end it with)
In gratitude,
Life

Allow yourself to bask in the glory and wonder of having actually accomplished all you dreamed you could do. Let yourself *feel* the appreciation of a grateful nation. If tears come, let them fall, and know that if this is a part of your soul purpose, you are destined to complete it before you leave the planet. Seeing it written down makes it so much more real, but also so much more possible.

4 Ask yourself in your heart of hearts, where truth alone resides, if you can say Yes to Life and Yes to this soul purpose as best you understand it today.

5   Sit quietly and let the magnitude of what you are committing to sink deeply into your heart and mind. No matter what comes up, keep saying Yes, softly and gently to yourself.

6   If No comes up instead, ask your heart if you can be willing to sit with these ideas, rereading your letter from Life each day. See if there is a portion you are willing to commit to; one idea that burns more brightly than the rest, and if you can commit only to that.

7   Remember that your Thinker may panic if it thinks it has to accomplish all you have set out here, because it already knows it doesn't know how to do it. Know, too, that your Knower already knows how to do all of this and more, because it goes to the fount of all knowledge and wisdom...the Great Knower itself, the One Mind that knows all things.

8   Ask that the wisdom of the Great Knower guide your every step, and claim that because It *always* says *Yes* and never No, that you do know what to do, and when and how to do it.

9   Write a clear, specific affirmation for each separate part of your commitment. Read them every morning or evening as part of your spiritual quiet time.

10 Give thanks *in advance* for the successful completion of all to which you have committed.

Rule 19

Smile At Life — Life Smiles At You. How you look at life is how life looks at you.

Physics teaches that for every action there is an equal and opposite reaction. Thus, through the law of cause and effect, each of our choices has tied to it an automatic consequence or reac-

> *"Taking responsibility means being aware of the multitude of choices you have in any given situation."*
> — Susan Jeffers, Ph.D., *Feel The Fear and Do It Anyway*

tion from an impersonal universe. Like a boomerang, the energy we send out through our thoughts and actions, both positive and negative, return to us automatically. The cumulative effect of our past choices forms the warp and woof of our lives today. We can look at life's inevitable inconveniences, screw-ups and pratfalls as unacceptable interruptions in our meticulously orchestrated days, or we can choose to find them (and ourselves in them) laughable, or even hysterically funny.

Coming out of the Nail Forum recently into a holiday packed parking lot, I could not see my car, but eventually located it behind a forty-foot-long semi delivering pallets of food to Del Taco. The remaining space between my car and the truck looked quite narrow, with the exit in one direction and the Del Taco drive-through in the other. But I am a *great* driver, and believe I can do just about *anything* with my car. (Aha, the Thinker at work!)

Unable to back in the direction needed in order to exit, I *thought* that there appeared to be enough room between the truck's tailgate and the drive-through to allow me to turn around and proceed safely out the exit. Getting there was easy—turning around was not. While I was busy jockeying back and forth and getting more stuck by the moment, a huge SUV pulled in behind me, blocking my exit! By then, my front tires were up on the metal tailgate of the semi, and my back tires were becoming intimately acquainted with the Del Taco menu board!

As we sat there staring at each other through our tinted car windows in a Western style face-off, the driver of the

It is not what life hands you, but how you handle what life hands you that makes all the difference.
— **Nancy B**

SUV was like, "Do something!", and I was like, "What?", and I started to laugh. Just then, the truck driver appeared, apologized, and began to untangle the mess. I responded through my laughter, "You're just doing your job," to which he looked genuinely surprised and replied, "Most people don't see it that way," and proceeded to help me get safely on my way.

So what were some of the "multitude of choices" available to me as I surveyed the situation? More importantly, how was I going to choose to respond emotionally, and what would be the automatic consequences of each of those choices?

As it was, both the truck driver and I left with big grins on our faces, and "feel good" endorphins running rampant through our brains and bodies, lowering our blood pressure, strengthening our immune system, thereby extending our life expectancy. I wish I could say that it is always that way—but it's not. However, by learning to connect the consequence, or response from the universe, through those around me to my choice of action, I have learned over time to make wiser choices and to accept responsibility for the consequences of the choices I have made. As a result, life smiles more often than frowns at me these days because I choose to smile at life.

When we allow ourselves to feel a kinship with those we meet in our daily lives, there is a greater sense of cooperation and a desire to work together for the mutual good of all concerned. A sense of well-being automatically follows such exchanges. Instead of reacting like adversaries, we can become team players, facing life's challenges together.

The opportunities to practice experiencing the consequences of our actions are presented to us daily; as when the line we *didn't* stand in sails along, while our line seems mired in mud, or when someone edges slowly in front of us in line while looking determinedly in the opposite direction as if we didn't exist. We are not designed to be doormats, and we have already learned that "stuffing it" does not work. If we choose to speak up, we find ourselves back at the choice regarding *how* we will speak and *from where*. Our Thinker, who feels threatened and out of control, wants to flex its muscles by putting down the line intruder. It might say something like, "Hello!!! I am standing here! Are you blind? The end of the line is back there!" If, however, we choose to allow a sense of kinship and its attendant desire toward cooperation to lead us to our Knower's wisdom, we might remember when we did the same thing (oh yes, we have!) and speak from our heart, with something like, "Excuse me. You seem to be in a hurry. I noticed that you stepped in front of me. Can I help you in any way?" You can't fool Mother Nature. If your comments—whatever they are—come from a genuine place of love and a desire to assist, the response will most likely be in kind. However, if the same words are spoken with sarcasm and a need to control, we can expect an equal response to come at us from the other person. Whatever the response, remember that you are responsible *only* for yourself, for *your* words and actions. Let others take responsibility for themselves.

We do not always recognize life's little instructions as the consequences of our actions because they do not always return to us from the same source. However, have you ever walked away from an unpleasant exchange feeling better-than-thou and oh-so-right straight into a doorjamb, or tripped over nothing, flat on your face? I have, and now I usually smile as I pick myself up, because I know I brought it on myself!

Thoughts that separate and divide us from those we meet, even in the most difficult situations, add to the violence in our world. Thoughts that unify us, that seek to get inside the other person's head and look out at the world through their eyes to try to understand where they are coming from, add to the peace. The Thinker divides, categorizes, compares, and then judges and finds fault, while the Knower, who is faultless, includes, honors the other's right to choose, and releases them to their own highest good.

Action Steps/Your Turn

1 Write at least six possible choices of action, both positive and negative, that were available to me when I discovered myself blocked in by the truck.

∽❷

_____

_____

_____

_____

_____

2 Write the probable automatic consequences of each of these choices.

∽❷ _____

_____

_____

_____

_____

_____

3 Remember a time recently when you made a less than positive choice, when you "lost it," and come up with at least four possible choices for that situation, including the ridiculous or outrageous. Allowing ourselves to think "outside the box" sometimes helps uncover the Knower's wisdom, which lies hidden within our hearts.

∽⊕

_____

_____

_____

_____

_____

4 Write the probable automatic consequences to each of these possible choices. Do not think too hard, just make them up! Out of your possible new choices, choose one along with its attendant consequence.

∽⊕

_____

_____

_____

_____

_____

Note: The following exercise will be done in silence. Please read it through completely before beginning. A pause is indicated by: —

Be sure you are comfortably seated, with your back well supported, so your body can relax. —

Take a deep breath, close your eyes, and move into the silence. —

Now, replay the entire scenario in your mind, replacing your former choice with the new one. —

Feel the other party or parties responding appropriately, in alignment with the new consequence. —

Notice any changes in your body/mind to this new, more harmonious scenario. —

Notice any release of tension and where you were holding it; in your diaphragm, neck or shoulders, face or forehead. —

Notice any changes in breathing patterns or heartbeat. —

Sit with it for a few minutes, perhaps expanding or editing your new scenario for an even more beneficial result for all involved. —

Notice how good it feels to be in your own relaxed body.

When you feel complete, return your attention to the present, and to the room in which you are seated.

Breathe deeply, stretch, and when you are ready, open your eyes.

Jot down some notes on this experience so you can refer to them again when you find yourself faced with another "situation" and another opportunity to make a choice.

ᐸᗘ

Remember: Your subconscious mind does not know the difference between a "real" and an imagined experience. It believes what you tell it implicitly, and acts on it with unlimited resources of power and creativity.

Rule 20

"Begin with the end in mind."

— Stephen Covey, *The 7 Habits
of Highly Effective People*

When I "believe and live" my life as though the Universe supports me, it does. When I believe and live as though it does not, it doesn't, always proving me, and my beliefs, right!

> *"There is a place within my belief system where I feel a connectedness with life's meaning, and that the universe supports me because I believe and live as though it does."*
> — Rev. Dr. Jesse Jennings

Recently, I needed to find a receipt from two years ago. During that period, I moved from our family home into a townhouse, downsizing enormously, letting go of a lifetime's accumulation of "important papers," furniture, etc. I released much of my husband's business papers and reorganized the file cabinet.

At first, I thought it was impossible and gave up without even looking for the receipt. Talk about trying to find a needle in a haystack! However, eventually I began to see where it might logically be, and set out today—*after* my morning's prayer connection to my Source—to either find it or release the need and let it go. In the first manila envelope I opened, I found another envelope indicating the types of receipts for which I was looking. Upon opening it, the specific receipt I was looking for was *open, on the very top*, as if waiting for me to find it!

These wonderful mini-miracles are happening to me so often these days that I have come to accept them as normal—"Oh yes, of course!"—though my awareness of being supported by a personal connection to my Source and my gratitude for its guidance and direction never wanes. I am just not so surprised anymore. In awe, yes, but not surprised.

About a year ago, when I was faced with so many decisions— whether to sell or not, to leave my place of employment and therefore my source of income, to move to another city and where, and how I would *ever* support myself—I wrote the following affirmation, which I memorized and use still today:

Since the One Mind is all-knowing and everywhere-present,
all my needs are known and provided for instantly and constantly
by my indwelling Source of limitless supply.

The word *affirm* means *to make firm.* When we speak our word, we are sending its energy out into the universe, which acts on it without question, returning to us the equivalent of our spoken word in form. When we speak of ourselves negatively—when we do not believe we have what it takes—the universe rewards us with evidence to prove we are right. When we "begin with the end in mind," as Henry Ford did in creating the first piston-driven engine (and as I did in finding my perfect new home), we *see* the desired end result so clearly, that no amount of negative feedback from the world can permanently alter our course or stop us dead in our tracks. We may stall from time to time, but our vision is so powerful, it will pull us back into action before long.

The beloved tree outside my window has willingly released every single leaf to the season of change called winter. Standing bare and bereft, naked in the winter wind, having let go of all the beauty it has gloried in throughout the year, it waits in silence for a future, yet unknown. While nothing appears to be happening on the *outside*, we know that indeed something important is taking place on the *inside*. The tree cannot grow any taller or broader than its root system, hidden within the earth. So the energy that, for most of the year, flows into a bountiful unfolding of the most majestic leafing of a tree I have ever seen, instead in winter, flows into strengthening and extending its unseen root system, so that an even more glorious foliage may appear in its own perfect divine right season, timing, and order.

It is important in the winter seasons of our lives to remember that though things may appear to have been stripped away—and we may even feel lifeless, as the tree appears to be—something is indeed taking place beneath the surface of our conscious mind, preparing us for the spring flowering and fruitage so certain to follow in its own perfect divine right season, timing, and order.

There are less hours of daylight and more hours of darkness in the winter, inviting us to turn within to our sacred space and find the solace we seek there. When the life we have known has been stripped away, or no longer satisfies, we have arrived, ready or not, at the changing of our seasons, and something must be released before the new, more satisfying and fulfilling experience can come into form. Releasing the old, familiar, comfortable lifestyle may challenge us to our very core, but doing so willingly creates a void, which Nature, in her infinite wisdom, rushes in to fill.

If we have been grateful for the activity, we must now learn to be grateful for its opposite, the incubation period, the R&R, which prepares us for the "future yet unknown," so that when it arrives, we will be ready! If you're like me, you probably prefer to know what's coming next so you can plan and prepare; but sometimes we are called upon to simply trust, and at times we find that is literally all we *can* do.

When I first met Barbara Martin, she was so withdrawn, I could hardly see who she was. With an outgoing husband and two young rambunctious sons, she rarely spoke, did not look you in the eye, and hid behind a lovely fall of chestnut hair. Colorless and silent, like the bare tree in winter, something important was taking place deep within her soul. We became friends in time, and her natural artistic talents and abilities began to bud and flower through meditation, class work, and spiritual counseling. A cellist with the Redlands Symphony Orchestra, she had a burning desire to teach music to children when the local school system's budget slashes forced elimination of all music from the curriculum. However, there was no money to pay a music teacher, so while her own family struggled financially, and with only the tiniest beginning buds of self-confidence, hard won through the daily connection with her Source, writing her goals and speaking her affirmations, she began taking her first baby steps toward fulfilling her dream. Starting with a handful of students and the recorder and violin, she taught children after school for whatever their parents could pay.

> *"Sometimes your only available transportation is a leap of faith"*
> — Rev. Margaret Shepherd

Today, four years later, she has applied for and received grants, worked with principals and PTAs at three schools (by whom she is now paid), and through the fundraising efforts and support of her community, has been able to purchase twenty violins, which are used by her more than forty students who perform regularly throughout the community. She knows what is needed to expand her program to meet the growing demands of parents and children who dream of playing an instrument, and of one day being part of a band or orchestra, and she goes after it.

To say that all this would have been impossible for the woman I met so many years ago would be a vast understatement. The full flowering of her spirit, her nonstop energy in pursuit of her goals, and her commitment to using her God-given talents and abilities in service to others, has taken her far beyond what she ever dreamed possible. Her transformation continues to unfold—but there is more.

> *"Discipline is the first stage. Learning a new task requires training your body to perform your thought's desire."*
> — Wayne Dyer, *The Power of Intention*

When she came to understand early on that it would be only through a Power greater than she was that she would be able to overcome her own lack of self-confidence in order to reach her goals, she made a deep commitment to daily spiritual practice. Over the years, she began to feel the loving Presence moving within her and speaking to or through her, and she set her intention to "be inspiration" and began writing down what she "heard" in what she called the "daily word." As requests grew for these daily writings, she began sending them to friends and family over the Internet.

Today, I received in the mail her first book of inspired daily messages from the Divine. Titled *Enter My Open Heart*, I pressed it to my own heart as I gave thanks to the One Creator for yet another dream fulfilled. To witness this transformation and to walk alongside a beloved one as they discover and open to their own God-given magnificence is a privilege no words can describe.

In a recent letter, Barbara wrote, "I will never forget the first time I counseled with you and...accepted that *I* might have to be the one to change. (Naturally, I wanted everyone around me to change so that I could be more comfortable.)" She wrote that I might not even recognize her today, since she has: cut her hair, had her "colors" done, and even visited the make-up counter at Nordstrom's. In addition, she has become a runner and joined Toastmasters. Barbara's new goals when we spoke were to run a 5K and to give her very first speech. She closed with, "It's like awakening to a whole new life, discovering the possibilities out there." To learn more about Barbara and her book, go to: **www.entermyopenheart.com.**

Everyone is born with this ability to connect with the Source, the One Creator of all that is, or ever will be, and through this *connection*, to make their dreams come true.

Action Steps/Your Turn

1 As suggested in Rule #11: *Establish a regular time and place for your spiritual practice, and stick to it.* Nothing else can bring you the greater good you desire...your "impossible dream."

2 Reread the quote on connection at the beginning of this Rule, write it on a 3x4 card, and carry it with you everywhere you go.

"...often My children turn to Me in time of disaster or trouble, but in time of joy they turn not. They hug the joy to their heart, forgetting that I am Joy also."
– Eva Bell Werber,
The Journey With the Master

3 Read it over ten times every morning and evening until you have memorized it and can feel the truth of it resonate in your heart.

4 Recognize that there is an Intelligent Power greater than you are at work in the universe, and that all of your creativity is the One Creator continuing to create *through you!* Acknowledge its Presence!

5 Establish a relationship with it. *Talk out loud.* Communicate your challenges, frustrations and disappointments, and ask for help. Yes, it may feel odd at first, but if you're not willing to state your needs clearly, how do you expect to receive the help you need, or to recognize it when it comes?

6 *Believe* that you, and your dreams, are being supported by this limitless Creative Source that wants you to succeed so that It may be more fully expressed on planet Earth.

7 Remember to share your accomplishments; your joys, as well as your sorrows, and acknowledge their Source, as well as the lovely "coincidences" that brought you exactly what you needed at exactly the moment you needed it!

8 Keep a daily journal and jot down something in it every day in conjunction with your practice. If nothing comes—write that. Write nonsense, write your frustrations, but write something every day.

Rule 21

Age Is a State of Mind.

Too young, or too old, it's all in our head, in the domain of the Thinker, while the Knower knows that time, as such, does not

> *"Do not tell me you are too old. Age is all imagination.Ignore years and they will ignore you."*
> — Ella Wheeler Wilcox

exist. We made it up! Humanity invented it as a way to get to the dentist on time, and then forgot that we created it, and so use it against ourselves as though it were an intractable fact!

Age is a state of mind and when we ignore the years, the years ignore us. Young people today, children and teens, are becoming successful entrepreneurs—recording, film, and TV stars and often zillionaires when most of us were still trying to figure out who was going to take us to the sock hop, or how to cover up our zits. There are no limits to what we can accomplish—*at any age*— unless, of course, we "Think" there are.

My dad was an extrovert. I guess that, coupled with a photographic mind, was what allowed him to rise above his dirt-poor beginnings and seventh-grade education to become an officer in the United States Navy. His classmates dubbed him The Arkansas Whiz Kid. He worked longer and harder than anyone else (he had to), took every course offered, and was first in every class except math. He continued to take courses by mail while at sea, spoke out against wrongdoing wherever he found it, regardless of personal cost, and as such was highly respected by the men who served under him.

In the late '20s, he began to sing and dance the Charleston during half times at the Army/Navy football games, and gained a reputation; so the sailors would chant, "We want Song-Bird, we want Song-Bird!" He was never famous, and never made a pot full of money, but he was one of the happiest, most contented, in-love-with-life people I have ever known. He would play his guitar and sing anytime, anywhere, whether people wanted to hear him or not—and usually, they did.

I remember throwing a huge holiday party for about seventy-five people. My husband, who wasn't into country music at the time, thought we should set up the musicians in our small 12x14 den (Daddy always had a following), leaving the very spacious and elegant living/dining room area for our other guests. Needless to say, nearly all seventy-five hung in the doorway, or leaned in the kitchen pass-through, because that was where the "action" was, and we were all having so much fun!

In his mid-eighties, he began having serious health challenges. The Navy doctors refused to give him the surgery he needed, saying he would not survive it, but he would not die. Eventually, his family doctor approved the procedure, and he struggled valiantly to recover. During the next five years he was at death's door six

> *"He's not tall or*
> *handsome*
> *it's plain to see*
> *as he sings and dances*
> *for you.*
> *His glory has faded*
> *But nobody sees.*
> *They see the love of my*
> *Daddy 'n me.*
> *The love of my Daddy*
> *'n me."*
>
> *Daddy 'n Me*, song by
> Nancy B

times, only to fight back to live another day.

During those difficult years, he still played and sang at every opportunity. When he wasn't too ill to get out of bed, he and my mother would be off; traveling, visiting friends, seeing the world, and loving every minute of it. It was during one of these trips that he was invited to sing at the Grand Old Oprey in Nashville, Tennessee. As pleased as he was with the invitation, his health would not permit it.

Years before, Mother and Dad had set Sunday evenings for regular phone calls to my brother and his wife, who lived all over the country and in faraway exotic locales. On the night before he died, Dad stood up and sang *Let the World Go Away* at their community center's potluck dinner. Later that night when Jim called, he asked, "How are you doing, Dad?" His answer tells more about him than words could ever say. He said,

"100%! No Complaints!"
. . . with all the energy of a twenty-year-old!

Six hours later, he was gone.

This from a man who was born into grinding poverty, was abused by his father, was sent by him as a child to pick cotton where he caught malaria, was in every major campaign in the Pacific in WWII, and struggled with painful medical problems much of his last five years on earth. In spite of all this, his view of life and his participation in it was, "100%! No Complaints!" One month short of his ninetieth birthday, he lived his life to the fullest, to his very last breath.

As extroverted as my father was, my introverted mother was talked into teaching hula lessons at eighty-five to the women in her mobile home park for their upcoming luau, then performed with them *for the very first time in public* (I have the video) when they discovered that they couldn't do it without her. With their encouragement and Daddy gone, she took lessons, learned new routines, and went on to dance with them at senior centers in the area.

The week before her passing, she requested a party with singing and dancing, and all her family and friends. When the evening arrived, she could not at first join us, but unable to resist the music, she was assisted to her chair where she held court, eyes closed, unable to speak, but with a lovely soft smile on her face. While my brother played the guitar and sang, and my sister-in-law and I danced the hulas we had all done together for so many years, Mother did the graceful hand movements in perfect rhythm to the island songs she knew and loved so well.

What is it that you have wanted so much to do? Have you convinced yourself that you are too young, or too old to learn something new, to start all over, or to be a beginner again?

This quote from *Tomorrow's God*, by Neale Donald Walsch, always moves me back into action whenever I feel discouraged, stuck, or depressed. In fact, it knocks me out!

"Hold nothing back.
Do not fear failure, and save nothing for later.
Do not hide your light under a bushel, but let it so shine that all may see the wonder of you, thus to know the wonder of themselves, for others see their possibility in the reality of you.
Be therefore, a model to the world."

We have something to learn from the youth today who fear nothing, and who have come to believe through the Internet that the whole world is their oyster and are proving more and more every day that they are right.

Age is a state of mind, and while the Thinker struggles with excess pounds, zits, wrinkles, or sags, the Knower dances in wild abandon in celebration of Life! We are here to explore, discover, and use the limitless opportunities available to us, and the limitless Power that backs them up. There are people today who are urgently seeking the exact gift that only you have to give. What are you waiting for? Whose permission do you need to step out in faith and live your dream?

In five years from now, you will still be five years older, whether you step out or not. You can do it! So why not go for it—today. Sure, you have missed opportunities, blown it, and messed up, that's all part of life; but you have also had some successes. People's lives have been changed for the better because of you! It's OK to acknowledge your screw-ups, and what you learned from them, but you must also acknowledge your wins!

Action Steps/Your Turn

1 List five wins or successes—things you have accomplished in the past year. They can be great or small. Size is not as important as how you felt at their completion.

̭

_____

_____

_____

2 Briefly jot down the one lack of success from the past year that you most regret.

̭

_____

_____

_____

3 Acknowledge what you learned from it. As long as you fight it, continuing to blame others, it saps your energy. The moment you accept the lesson it came to offer, it loses its power over you, and sets you free to move on to the next accomplishment.

4 Where do you want to be five years from now? List the changes you desire to see in your life five years from today. Make them as simple and clear as possible.Examples: go back to school, pay off credit cards, be debt-free (except for mortgage payments), exercise daily; create a systematic savings plan, etc.

∽❥ _____

_____

_____

_____

_____

5 Send five thank you notes to people who assisted you in some way during the past year. Try to pick people you would not normally think to thank, like your dentist or banker. If it feels uncomfortable, that's OK. Your simple note of acknowledgement can really make someone's day.

6 Write a thank you note to yourself from someone whose life you touched this year. Speak as the other person, coming from the heart, and sign their name. Mail it to yourself.

7 When you receive it, read it, and really take it in. Don't let yourself laugh it off, or set it aside. Let it touch you deeply, and acknowledge the good you have done in the world. Pause and give thanks to your Source for the opportunity to touch and be touched by life.

Rule

Lift Up and Be Lifted. As we lift up another, we too are lifted.

When I pray for you, the words of encouragement I speak, acknowledging the Presence and Power within you and available to you in every moment to rise above whatever challenge you may be facing—the peace, serenity, and divine right action I call upon in your name, flow first through me. I cannot help but feel uplifted when I recall to mind the truth about you; that you can never be separated from your Source, and that all the wisdom, strength, health, and abundance you will ever need are already yours, since the Source within you is forever whole, complete, and rests at the point of harmony, peace, and joy. Therefore, whatever *appears* to be less than good in your experience may be a fact, and we do not deny its existence, but it is not the ultimate truth about you, or anyone else, and is therefore passing through; it has not come to stay.

> *"It is one of the beautiful compensations of life that no one can sincerely try to help another without helping himself."*
> — Mark Twain & Charles Dudley Warner, *The Gilded Age*

As I recall each of these truths and speak them for you with conviction that comes from a deep Knowing, a sense of peace and gratitude flow through me, for I can feel the truth of it resonate in my soul and know that, in spite of all appearances, it is done! It may take time to come into form, but the seed has been planted, and it must come to pass.

Miracles occur when we allow the wisdom of our inner Knower to guide us to truths we did not know we knew. We hear ourselves saying things we never thought of and know it is coming from the fount of Infinite Knowledge, far beyond our own individual minds.

You have the ability to call forth a healing, or revealing for yourself or another, not because of any personal power, but because the One Power that flows through all things also flows through you. All faiths call upon this same Power, by whatever name they choose. Healings have been accomplished through prayer in every faith and through no particular faith at all. Two examples come to mind.

The minister of the first church my husband and I attended related an instantaneous "healing" that took place when he was moving his family to Southern California where he had accepted a position in a local church. He was pulling a trailer loaded down with all their worldly possessions up the infamous Grapevine, that grueling climb from the desert floor to 4,000 plus feet on the 5 Freeway when his engine died and his brakes failed. As he began rolling backwards down this steep mountain grade, he called out loud to his Higher Power with just two words: "HELP ME!" No time for formal prayers, no time for a prayer hotline. His wife and children were in the car, rolling backwards, out of control, he did not know what to do, and he needed help...Instantly!

In that moment, the driver's door flew open, a burly man shoved him over, jumped in, and expertly steered the car and trailer safely to a complete stop at the side of the road. Somehow, this truck driver had seen what was happening, was able to stop his rig, and run to the car before some horrific accident could occur.

How was this possible? Did time stand still long enough for this angel to step in?

Was it good luck, a coincidence? You can call it that if you choose. I prefer to call it answered prayer. The title of our minister's lecture on that Sunday was "Being Prayed Up Ahead," so that in those moments when help is needed instantly, it is not necessary to *introduce* ourselves to our Higher Power—we have already established a relationship through our daily spiritual practice. This Power is available to all of us, all of the time, not just in emergencies. We can call upon it in our little daily challenges and be led to simple solutions with amazing ease rather than trying to figure it out on our own.

Praying together is one of the most powerful spiritual tools we possess. It is so easy for us to see and claim the truth for another...the divine right solution to whatever their concerns might be. It seems we cannot always so easily see our own answers to sticky problems, but our prayer partners can. Praying together and focusing on another's immediate concerns also helps to put our own challenges into perspective. What we place our attention on, and therefore our energy, tends to grow. If we do not watch our thoughts carefully, we can feed energy to the negative situations in our lives unknowingly, until they feel unmanageable, when in fact they are not.

After two weeks of almost steady, pounding rain, including dark, overcast days and several doors seeming to close in my face, I became discouraged and depressed about life in general. The book writing came to a standstill; my computer froze, causing me to lose several days work; and the garage door broke with my car inside! I was *stuck*, and Life was giving me all the evidence I needed to confirm my self-made affirmation. You know the one: "Nobody loves me. I'm going out in the garden and eat some worms."

Therefore, I was in a dark mood yesterday when I pulled into a parking space outside my voice teacher's studio. Somehow, my tires missed the cement-parking block and when I tried to back up, it would not move. No matter how I turned the tires or rocked the car back and forth, it would not let me go. Once again, Life offered up *concrete evidence* that, "Yep! You are definitely *stuck!*" and I started to laugh. I was hung up on the *only bolt* that stuck up from any of the concrete blocks in the whole parking lot! It was as if the Universe was trying to tell me: "Life is just not that serious. Lighten up!"—and I did. In that very moment, I gave it all up. I just let go and the sun began to shine inside me once again. Even though I had an important appointment, which I would now be late for as I waited for AAA to pull me out, I totally relaxed and enjoyed each moment of the day from that time on. (PS: I am writing again.)

> *"More things are wrought by prayer than this world dreams of."*
> – Alfred Lord Tennyson

I have been blessed to have had several dedicated prayer partners through the years. Esther, my current prayer partner and I have an agreement to speak weekly on Mondays, Wednesdays, and Fridays at 7:00 AM. Years ago, I was very strict regarding the exact days and times we would speak. Now, after twenty-five years of disciplined daily spiritual practice, I am more relaxed, realizing that whenever we are able to pray together is the perfect right time.

It is such a privilege to be asked to pray with someone for the divine right solution to his or her problems. At the same time, hearing someone speak faith-filled words regarding our own challenges lifts clouds of doubt and fear, allowing us to see solutions that were there all along.

Just being willing to ask someone for prayer is half the battle. Our ego wants to believe (and wants others to think) that we have all the answers and do not need anyone else. It requires humility to say simply, "I need help." Nothing is too small, shameful, or shocking to share with another trusted soul in prayer, and to take together to the One, who knows all things anyway.

When we sit together in prayer, whether in person or on the phone, it is important to open our hearts, listen and speak from this heart of love, without judgment or blame.

"No problem can be solved at the same level that created it."
— Albert Einstein

We must come up higher, to tap into the wisdom of the Infinite Knower, who reveals to us exactly what we need to know when we open ourselves to receive it. "I don't know" is a powerful place to come from, because even the Creator itself cannot fill a cup or a mind that is already full of itself, and therefore closed to new ideas or ways of seeing or doing things.

ACTION STEPS/YOUR TURN

1   Practice praying aloud if you have never tried it before. Just speak naturally, as you would to a trusted friend in sharing your concerns and your need for guidance and right answers.

2   If you do not already have a prayer partner, consider first being one, and then finding the perfect prayer partner for you. Ask to be guided to the right person, and you will be.

3   If this is your first experience in praying for another person, say so. Share any concerns you may have, and invite the other person to do the same.

4   Discuss confidentiality with your prayer partner. In order for your prayer time together to be fruitful, you must both be able to trust your partner implicitly.

5   Agree on the days and times you will speak. Try it for a week or two, and be ready to modify it as your prayer pattern becomes more firmly established.

6   Select days and times when you expect to have quiet and privacy. You might even consider going to your car for a few minutes if you are at work.

7   Keep it short and to the point. This is not a social visit. It has a sacred purpose, and in order for it to serve that high purpose, you must honor and respect each other's time, as well as each other's prayer requests.

8 End in prayer. Do not dilute the energy of the prayer by rehashing the event for which you have just prayed, or by jumping back into your "to do" list too quickly.

9 Sit quietly for a moment or two, allowing the loving energy of your connection to your Source to wash through your body and mind, releasing all tension and leaving peace in its place.

Rule 23

Life Goes On.

Whether we are for it or against it, winning or losing, celebrating or mourning, what we notice about life is

> *"Be assured, life is always a forward motion."*
> – Edie Jurmain, R.Sc.P.

that it goes on. Sometimes we feel like it is spinning out of control and we'd like to slow it down or get off the planet for awhile to rest or regroup, but that is not life's way. Life is forever a forward motion. It cannot stop or go backward to give us time to "find ourselves" or to change the decisions we've made in order to alter the consequences we are now experiencing.

The point is that whether you were the prom queen, star quarterback, or a high school drop out, *IT'S OVER* and hanging onto our successes keeps us just as stuck as hanging onto what we call our failures. Some of today's most successful entrepreneurs dropped out of school. So what? Hiding behind our past—whatever it was—is just an excuse for not participating in life *today*!

One thing I know for sure: We will never pass this way again. This day, today, for better or worse, will never come again, and time has a way of moving ahead whether we choose to go along for the ride or not. Whatever you dream of doing in your life,

DO IT NOW!

SAY IT NOW!

LIVE IT NOW!
BELIEVE IN IT NOW!
MAKE A DECISION AND TAKE ACTION ON IT NOW...
TODAY!

Remember Rule #1:
IT ALL BEGINS IN THE MIND

Marianne Williamson wrote in her new book, *The Gift of Change,*

*"Once you know that everything in your life arises from consciousness
you start looking pretty closely at what goes on between your ears.
Change that and you change your world."*

Well, here we are at the end of our journey together. Thank you
for participating in creating this fantastic adventure. You see, this
book would never have been written if you, and others like you,
had not been seeking solutions to some of Life's sticky problems
as presented in these Rules for the Game of Life. It would never
have been called forth into form through me. I pray that applying
these Rules to your own life has changed the way you think about
yourself and your dreams, because this is not the end—it's just the
beginning.

The same Creative Power that brought this book into form is
flowing through you right now, in this very moment. It is
Limitless in its ability to *do*, but it has no volition of its own. *You*
must give it the direction in your life that you desire. You do that
through the thoughts you think, the dreams you dream, the goals
you set, and the actions you take on them. *If you keep doing what
you've always done, you'll always get what you've always got!* If you

want to accomplish more, if you want to live your dreams, you must *change the way you think* and change your inner talk about yourself. Be vigilant. Guard the doorway to your mind, and do not allow negative thoughts to demean or limit you in any way.

Remember, hard or easy, big or small are our ideas. The Creator of all that is knows nothing of those things. If you believe you can, you can; if you believe you can't, you can't. It's that simple. It's so simple, in fact, that we ignore it, thinking that if it were really that simple, everyone would do it. It is simple, but it is not easy to believe in yourself and your dreams when the whole world may call you a fool. It takes discipline, persistence, hard work, and faith in a Power greater than you are to bring it about. So, most don't bother to apply these simple Rules that you now know because they don't believe it can be done. But you are not one of those disbelievers. You have already set your intention to *believe* through the work you have done in completing the exercises in this book; through the goals you have set and the affirmations you have written to support those goals! So, here is an affirmation to help you put your plans into action:

> *I believe in my ability to co-create my life and my dreams*
> *with the Limitless Power of the One Creator*
> *within me who wants me to succeed!*

No one can withhold your good from you—your success, your dreams, your vision. It is yours for the taking, but you must claim it, believe it, act as though it is already done, and then go after it with all the energy, enthusiasm, joy, and gratitude you can muster. It was planted in your heart by the Divine; therefore, everything you will ever need has already been provided. Oh, there will be tough days, challenges, and setbacks; times when you will want to throw in the towel and walk away, back to where it was more comfortable and safe. But those are simply messages from the Universe, asking whether you *really* want it or if you're just kidding yourself. It's your opportunity to recommit, to clarify and strengthen your intention, to go back to your affirmation regarding this goal (if you didn't write one, do it now) and repeat it silently, to yourself, *all day long*. Soon the clouds will lift. Someone will seem to drop out of the sky (that's your Source, the Creator at work) at exactly the right moment, with exactly the right answer, and you will be off and running again.

These Rules of the Game of Life represent my life experiences and my particular point of view. Yours will be different. However, all people everywhere want essentially the same things when it comes down to the bottom line. We want a connection with our Creator, to know that we are never alone, that we belong, and that our contributions make a difference in the world. We want health and well-being for ourselves and our families. We want someone to love, who loves us back. A peaceful co-existence in community with others and in our world, and a meaningful, purpose-filled life so that at the end of our days we can know that we faced life head on, took what came our way, and made the best of it. Not that we did it all, but that we loved Life and the people in it, that we gave it everything we had, and that Life loved us back. In the end...

Life is a Game,
and it's not about winning or losing, it's about
how we play the game.

GOAL SETTING

After completing your list of ten goals to which you are willing to commit, write them here. *Read them daily, morning and night, with feeling*, allowing them to sink deeply into your subconscious mind. Then release them to the Creator of all that is, or ever will be. You do not need to know where your greater good, the funds, or the contacts you need to bring them about will come from. That is not your job. Your job is to create the "what," then turn it over to the Creator who wants you to succeed and who will create the "how." Outlining where and how our good will come to us tends to put limits on the limitless. Greater good is in store for you than you can even dream.

1 _____

_____

_____

2 _____

_____

_____

3 _____

_____

_____

4 _____

_____

_____

5 _____

_____

_____

6 _____

_____

_____

7 _____

_____

_____

8 _____

_____

_____

9 _____

_____

_____

10 _____

_____

_____

YOUR PLEDGE

I, _____ , acknowledge the Presence and Power of the One Creator of all that is or ever will be right here where I am, acting in me, through me, as me, from whom these ideas for my greater good arose. I do here and now commit to fulfilling them, each and every one. I further commit to watering them daily with my faith and gratitude, knowing that having done my part, I can let go and let the Creator itself do the greater part. My heart sings in gratitude and joy, knowing it is done.

Name: Date:

GOAL SETTING
REWRITES & ADDITIONS

Use these pages to rewrite or add new goals as you complete those on the preceding pages. Congratulations! You are well on your way to creating the life of your dreams. Give yourself permission to cancel goals that no longer fit your new direction, but be certain that you are not being controlled by ego fears, laziness, or procrastination. Commit yourself to living your life with purpose and passion, and stick to it. Be patient, but be persistent. Remember, your word has power. Use it only for the good of yourself and of others. Never use it to criticize yourself or another.

"Everything you are against weakens you. Everything you are for empowers you."
— Dr. Wayne W. Dyer, *The Power of Intention*

_____

_____

_____

_____

_____

_____

_____

Rewrites & Additions, ctd.

Formula for Success

1 Admit there is a problem. State it briefly here.
☞

_____

_____

_____

2 Ask for help. If you are stuck, call a friend you can trust to listen without judgment and talk it out.

3 Accept your part in helping to create it (your Thinker hates this). Write briefly about how you contributed to creating the problem. Be honest, do not leave anything out, or be tempted to shift the blame to another.

4 Be willing to hear the answer, even if it feels uncomfortable or scary.

5 Make a definite commitment to act upon the answer you receive by a specific day and time, and then sign it, creating a sacred contract with your Higher Power. If you need support to be certain you will follow through and keep your word, call your friend who was willing to listen and support you earlier and ask them to hold you accountable.

Name:　　　　　Date:　　　　　Day:　　　　　Time:

Resources

Neale Donald Walsch, *Tomorrow's God*. (Atria Books, Simon & Schuster, Inc., 2004) **www.HumanitysTeam.com**

Julia Cameron, *The Artists Way*. (Jeremy P. Tarcher, Putnam Books, New York, 1992)

William Paul Hansen, R.C.L., *Hope Heals*. (Literary Press, Newport Beach, CA, 2004) **www.noparkinsons.net**

Ruby Nelson, *The Door of Everything*. (DeVorss & Company, 1963)

Barbara Martin, Enter *My Open Heart*. (Author House, 2004) **www.entermyopenheart.com**

Susan Jeffers, Ph.D., *Feel The Fear And Do It Anyway*. (Fawcett Columbine: New York, 1987, Published by Ballantine Books)

Dr. Wayne W. Dyer, *The Power of Intention*. (Hay House, Carlsbad, CA, 2004)

Eva Bell Werber, *The Journey with the Master*. (Devorss & Company, Marina Del Rey, CA, 1950)

Don Miguel Ruiz, *The Four Agreements*. (Amber-Allen Publishing, Inc., San Rafael, CA, 1997)

John Randolph Price, *The Abundance Book*. (Hay House, Inc., Carlsbad, CA, 1987)

ABOUT THE AUTHOR

A student of life and living, Nancy B is a born entertainer. Her empathy with and compassion for those struggling through challenges has led her to such diverse endeavors as being a Big Sister at L.A. Juvenile Hall, to entertaining our troops in hospitals and in the field. Acting, singing, and dancing since she was three, she retired in 1990 from SAG and AFTRA to pursue her spiritual studies. You can still catch her in reruns of some of your favorite shows, such as *Little House on the Prairie, Dynasty,* and *Fame.*

A dynamic and compelling speaker and teacher, Nancy empowers others with passion and humor to fulfill their lifelong dreams. Having transformed her own life from one of fear and self-sabotage to one of selfless service, she teaches by example how to overcome self-made limitations through faith in an indwelling Power greater than we are. Her heart-to-heart connection with her audience—whether onstage, in her book, or at seminars— makes each individual believe that she is speaking only to them.

An ordained minister in a trans-denominational philosophy, Nancy followed her inner guidance and returned to the San Fernando Valley area following the death of her husband. There, she rediscovered her first love, the stage, and has appeared in two theatrical productions since returning. When she is not acting, speaking, teaching, or writing, you can find Nancy enjoying her four adult children and their families: twelve grandchildren and three great-grandchildren, all of whom live in Southern California.